# The Catholic Parish

# The Catholic Parish

## Hope for a Changing World

*Robert J. Hater*

Paulist Press
New York/Mahwah, N.J.

Cover design by Cindy Dunne
Book design by Lynn Else

Library of Congress Cataloging-in-Publication Data

Hater, Robert J.
    The Catholic parish : hope for a changing world / Robert J. Hater.
        p.    cm.
    Includes bibliographical references.
    ISBN 0-8091-4281-3 (alk. paper)
    1. Pastoral theology—Catholic Church.  2. Parishes.  I. Title.

BX1913.H315  2004
254 .02—dc22

                                                        2004013309

Published by Paulist Press
997 Macarthur Boulevard
Mahwah, New Jersey 07430

www.paulistpress.com

Printed and bound in the
United States of America

# Contents

Preface .................................................................ix
Acknowledgments ..............................................xiii

Introduction ..........................................................1

PART ONE:
*Refocusing the Vision—Parishes: Past and Present* ..........7
  1. Today's Parishes at a Crossroad ..............................9
     Parishes: The Way They Were ...............................10
     Changes in Society, Changes in Parishes ...............11
     Historical Crossroads in U.S. Parishes...................14
     Pastoral Suggestions ............................................19
  2. Facing the New Crossroad ....................................21
     Shifting Theological and Pastoral Perspectives .......22
     Facing the New Crossroad ....................................24
     Internal Dynamics Facing Parish Life ...................27
     Pastoral Suggestions ............................................41
  3. Centering on People's Needs...................................44
     Catholic Identity.................................................45
     Addressing People's Needs...................................47
     Recreating the Parish...........................................50
     Pastoral Suggestions ...........................................55

PART TWO:
*Grounding the Vision—Evangelization* ........................59

4. Evangelization: The Heart of Parish Life
   and Ministry..........................................................61
   The Meaning of Evangelization ...........................63
   Evangelization and the Kingdom.........................66
   Evangelization and Ministry.................................71
   Evangelization: The Responsibility of
   the Entire Christian Community ...........................74
   Evangelization: Family, Parish, and Work .............75
   Pastoral Suggestions .............................................80

5. Evangelization and the Four Pillars
   of Parish Life.........................................................82
   The Four Pillars: Mission, Members, Ministry,
   and Management....................................................83
   Pastoral Suggestions .............................................102

PART THREE:
*Living Out the Vision—*
*Chief Aspects of Evangelizing Ministry* ........................105

6. Catechetical Ministry ............................................107
   Focusing Parish Catechesis ...................................109
   Dimensions of Catechesis ....................................120
   Catechetical Personnel..........................................125
   Pastoral Suggestions .............................................128

7. Liturgical Ministry ...............................................133
   The Meaning of Liturgy .......................................134
   Challenges to Liturgy ...........................................141

Enhancing Parish Liturgy ....................................148

Pastoral Suggestions ...........................................153

8. Service Ministry...............................................157

Parish Ministry and Jesus' Call to Serve..............159

Social Ministry in the Family and Society.............162

Pastoral Suggestions ...........................................168

PART FOUR:

*Realizing the Vision—The World and the Parish:*
*Present and Future*...............................................173

9. Challenging a Parish's Vision............................175

Society's Basic Orientation ................................178

Aspects of American Society..............................179

Pastoral Suggestions ........................................188

10. Managing the Parish's Vision...........................191

A Parish's Fundamental Orientation, Style,
and Mission.....................................................193

A Parish's Mission Statement............................199

The Parish Planning Process .............................205

Pastoral Suggestions ........................................211

11. Refocusing Parish Ministries through
Rites of Passages.............................................213

Meeting People's Basic Spiritual Needs................215

Key Life Moments and Sacramental Ministry ......217

Key Life Moments and Extra-Sacramental
Ministry..........................................................225

Pastoral Suggestions ........................................232

Bibliography.........................................................240

*I dedicate this book with love and*
*appreciation to my mother,*
Olivia L. Hater

Mom,
When I was a child,
you taught me to pray,
instructed me about God,
and helped me appreciate my parish, St. William's.
When I became an adult,
you continued to reflect God's love
and to support me in my ministry.
In your ninety-first year of life,
your faith, wisdom, and intelligence
bless and encourage me.

Thanks for your love and care,
and your willingness to read this manuscript
and comment on it.
May God bless you!
I love you very much.
Bob

# Preface

After I had written this dedication, Mom became very sick on the feast of the Epiphany, January 6, 2002, and on Good Friday, March 29, 2002, my best friend and mentor died peacefully and returned to God.

Following her death, I wrote this testimony to her life and holiness from her children.

## In Memoriam

On the last day when our mother was fully conscious, she sat in her hospital room on the fourteenth floor of Good Samaritan Hospital with her children Tom, Joan, Mary Ann, and Bob. At one point Mom peered past the image of Mary and Jesus painted on the window outside her room. She said, "I feel like I am on a mountain." Indeed, Mom *was* on a mountain—a spiritual one. Her remark recalls the time that Jesus went up on a mountain and spoke the Beatitudes, which were proclaimed at her Mass of Christian Burial.

In the days preceding her death, as the family kept vigil around her hospital bed, we discussed how the Beatitudes captured Mom's spirit. When we gently sponged Mom's gums to keep them moist, we imagined Mom's own gentle touch when we were sick or troubled. As we reminisced, we saw how fully she lived the Beatitudes. We also recalled my father's experience during his last illness. He described an out-of-body experience he had as a set of steps, each inscribed with a Beatitude, that he had to ascend to reach the Light.

When Mom died on Good Friday, March 29, 2002, at age ninety-one, pneumonia had taken her body, but she had never really grown old. Up to the moment she breathed her last, her spirit remained as vibrant as the day she entered this world. She exemplified the Beatitudes throughout her life. Mom's simple, unencumbered life filled her husband, her children, her grandchildren, and her great grandchildren with joy. No unkind word or cutting remark ever came from her lips. Even in her final suffering, the nurses and hospital staff repeatedly told us, "She never complains." Instead, encouragement and affirmation bespoke her greatness.

What is greatness? It comes from who we are, not what we do. Mom always reflected a free, inner-directed spirit. Our family remembers her stories, like her going alone at age eight to the wedding of a Jewish neighbor, at a time when Catholics did not do such things. When Mom reached the eighth grade, she had read every book in the local public library appropriate for her age. But after she was awarded a four-year scholarship to college, she declined it, choosing instead to get a job to support her immigrant mother and family. Years later, we would recall her saying, "If I had accepted that college scholarship, I would not have married your father, and you would not be here. Instead, I stressed education in our family. For me, seeing every one of my children and grandchildren with a college education is reward in itself." To the day that Mom went to the hospital for the final time, it was not unusual for a family member to ask her how to spell a word, correct English grammar, or critique a new book that one of her children was writing.

Mom never drove an automobile. She never joined an organization, preferring instead the wisdom gleaned from going to church, reading, meditating on nature's beauty, creating new recipes, working hard at home, enjoying the companionship of her faithful dog, Hanna, and giving total priority to her family. She loved to watch the "Reds" even when they lost. Her name never appeared in a newspaper. She never wrote a book.

And yet, Mom found real greatness. She was a truly liberated woman—free, strong, and up-to-date, yet kind, patient, and good. She never felt alone. She never felt sorry for herself. Her simplicity, wisdom, intellectual brilliance, and lived Catholic faith made her a beacon of confidence and hope. She inspired generations of children to see the importance of education and to know that the really good life is possible. At her funeral liturgy, we celebrated a woman who lived life in a complete, consistent, compassionate, and courageous way. Mom is now with Dad, hearing the words spoken in Matthew's Gospel, "Rejoice and be glad, for your reward will be great in heaven."

In this book I also honor the women who worked with me to begin and develop the Adult Spirituality Institute, namely, Karen Berry (deceased), Mary Frances Clauder, Allie Maggini, Bonnie Peterson, and Susan Tew.

I also express my special thanks to the following, who read this manuscript and offered valuable comments to improve it—Msgr. David Sork, Mrs. Karen Berry, Mrs. Momi Bolan, Rev. John Civille, Sr. Jeanette Jabour, OP, Rev. Dr. Annemarie Kidder, Rev. James McDougall, Ms. Mary Sue O'Donnell, Rev. Paul Rehling, Rev. Ted Kosse, and Mrs. Nancy Stagnaro. I am particularly grateful to Rev. Joseph Scott, CSP, and Paul McMahon, my editors at Paulist Press, for their valuable help in finalizing this book.

# Acknowledgments

I gratefully acknowledge material taken from the following sources:

*A Family in Church and Society,* © 1998 United States Conference of Catholic Bishops, Inc., Washington, DC. Used with permission. All rights reserved.

*Catechism of the Catholic Church,* © 1994 & 1997 United States Conference of Catholic Bishops, Inc., Washington, DC. Used with permission. All rights reserved.

*Catholic Evangelization: The Heart of Ministry* by Robert J. Hater, © 2002, Harcourt Religion Publishers, Dubuque, Iowa. Used with permission. All rights reserved.

*Catholicism USA* by Bryan T, Froehle and Mary L. Gautier, © 2000, Orbis Books, Maryknoll, NY. Used with permission. All rights reserved.

*Code of Canon Law, Latin-English Edition, New English Translation,* Canon Law Society of America, CSLA Publications, Washington, DC, 1999. Used with permission. All rights reserved.

*Excellent Catholic Parishes* by Paul Wilkes, © 2001, Paulist Press, Mahwah, New Jersey. Used with permission. All rights reserved.

*General Directory for Catechesis (GDC),* © 1997 United States Conference of Catholic Bishops, Inc.,

# Introduction

Today's parish offers a beacon of hope for future Catholics. It is primed to create new directions for priests and lay leaders to teach the good news of Jesus Christ. The past two generations saw shifts in the orientation of Catholic parishes, as unprecedented changes occurred in pastoral ministry, organizational style, and management. Today, many parishes have excellent catechesis, revitalized liturgies, multiple adult faith formation opportunities, vibrant youth ministries, a commitment to hospitality, and a deep concern for social justice. The need for spiritual renewal and prayer, benchmarks for parish growth, roots these ministries. Conscious of the need to stress hospitality, Catholic parishes offer great hope to society.

The parish of today is still changing, and the parish of yesteryear is gone forever. No longer will a pastor, like the one of my childhood, guide a parish for twenty or thirty years. No longer will a legion of nuns assist a pastor in his ministry. No longer will the laity sit back and dutifully follow each directive of the pastor or bishop. No longer will Mass be celebrated in Latin, but in the language of the people. Today, few religious sisters minister in parishes. Less than 50 percent of registered Catholics attend weekly Mass. The priest shortage approaches a critical mass as some parishes close. Parishes have difficulty attracting young people to Sunday liturgies, and women struggle to find their place in the Church.

Nonetheless, tomorrow's parish promises to be more vital than ever. Catholics look to the parish for support and spiritual ministry. They need help with their children and seek wisdom in coping with society's pressures. Our world and our Church are changing, as parishes embark on an uncertain journey. People need hope and assurance that life means more than the superficiality that they often witness in secular society. They look to their parishes to help them deepen their spiritual roots. During times like this, great opportunities exist to minister to people's spiritual needs.

The parish is primed to respond to such challenges. Its mission and ministry has been clarified during the past two generations. Ministerial leaders recognize the parish as a community of people who are called by the Lord to be disciples. Most parishes have adequate managerial systems to cope with complex issues facing them. They are in a strong position to respond to the Lord's call to minister.

Today's parishes need a vision and new directions. This book aims at helping them in their mission to proclaim the good news of God's love and forgiveness, as Jesus taught it and the Catholic tradition interprets it. This mission focuses on praying, learning God's Word, celebrating God's presence in the sacraments, and serving others.

This book is intended for those interested in making their parish a more faith-filled community. For this reason, it includes real-life stories, pastoral experiences, church directives, theological conclusions, managerial perspectives, and pastoral suggestions. These are blended into a holistic approach, which addresses the complex challenges facing parishes.

*The Catholic Parish* presumes a close link among the parish, diocese, and universal church. It sees each of these as mutually supportive of the rest. Under a pastor's leadership, the parish ministers to a particular community while reaching beyond it to the broader Church and world. This book concentrates on the parish itself, but presumes close connections with the entire Church.

No one model exists for every parish. With the movement toward larger parishes and the influx of various ethnic populations, needs vary from parish to parish. Since today's parishes differ in size, ethnic composition, and orientation, it is not possible to identify any one best parish model. This book addresses key dimensions of any faith-filled parish. It maintains that Catholic vitality begins in the family and is fostered on the parish level. When parishes are strong, the broader Church thrives. When its ministry extends beyond its local boundaries, the parish is strengthened and the entire Catholic community is enriched.

The book is divided into four parts with eleven chapters. Pastoral Suggestions to enhance parish ministry are offered at the conclusion of each chapter. Part One, "Refocusing the Vision," discusses the parish: past and present. Chapter One describes today's parishes as standing at a crossroads. It examines the parish of yesteryear, changes in society, changes in the Church, and historical crossroads of United States parishes. Chapter Two looks at how our current parishes face this a crossroad. It describes shifting theological and pastoral perspectives that challenge parish life. Chapter Three concentrates on a parish's members. It stresses Catholic identity, addressing peoples' needs, and recreating the parish.

Part Two, "Grounding the Vision," considers evangelization and the four pillars of parishes. Chapter Four concentrates on evangelization as the foundation of effective parish ministry. It looks at the meaning of evangelization, evangelization and ministry, and evangelization as the responsibility of the entire Christian community. Then it discusses evangelization in the family, workplace, and parish.

Chapter Five considers evangelization and the four pillars that underpin effective parishes. These pillars are a parish's members, mission, ministry, and management. Since each is essential, if one is weak, ministry suffers. A vibrant parish unifies them into a harmonious blend. Mission, the heart of parish vision, comes alive when related to the needs of parish members. This happens through ministry. Management refers to practical ways that parish leaders organize a parish's mission and ministry.

Part Three, "Living Out the Vision," treats the chief aspects of evangelizing ministry, namely, Word, worship, and service. Chapter Six concentrates on parish catechetical ministry, as it focuses on catechesis, dimensions and elements of catechesis, and catechetical personnel. It discusses adult faith formation, ministry with families, and youth ministry. Chapter Seven looks at the role of liturgy in the evangelization process. It stresses the importance of connecting liturgical actions with core needs of parishioners by discussing the meaning of the liturgy, internal and external challenges to liturgy, and enhancing parish liturgy. Christian service or social ministry is emphasized in Chapter Eight. It considers parish ministries and Jesus' call to serve, stresses the need for a parish to encourage social ministries to family and society, and offers suggestions to enhance family and service ministries.

Part Four, "Realizing the Vision," treats the parish: present and future. Chapter Nine discusses how society challenges a parish vision. It looks at important aspects of American society and emphasizes that God is found in the midst of society. Chapter Ten considers how the parish manages the vision. It treats the parish's orientation, style, mission, mission statement, and planning process. Chapter Eleven offers ways to refocus a parish's vision and ministries in light of the realities of the time. It concentrates on meeting people's basic spiritual needs, aiming at the core of life, and ministering during rites of passage. Key life moments and both sacramental and extra-sacramental ministry are addressed. Suggestions are offered on how to revitalize a parish's sacramental life and to become more sensitive to key life moments, when people are open to hear God's word. Rites of passage, like getting a driver's license, going to college, moving out of one's home, losing a job, having a miscarriage, are treated. Finally, the chapter offers a checklist for parishes to evaluate their ministry in light of the eighteen traits common to excellent parishes, offered by Paul Wilkes in his book *Excellent Catholic Parishes.*

Since every parish is different, various models exist for effective parish ministry. This book suggests a vision for parishes that goes beyond a parish's size, ethnic composition, and geographical location. By centering on Jesus' teaching, Catholic tradition, and basic human needs, it offers parishes a focus for today's world. When reading this book, you are invited to reflect on your previous parish experiences, considering how your parish has blessed you and how you can make your present parish a more effective vehicle to praise God, hear Jesus' word, celebrate it, and serve your brothers and sisters.

This book is written primarily from a Latin (Western) Church viewpoint. Although many points relate in a common way to parishes of all Catholic Traditions in union with Rome, life in Eastern Catholic parishes can often differ in virtue of their different Traditions.

PART ONE

*Refocusing the Vision—*
*Parishes: Past and Present*

# 1.

# *Today's Parishes at a Crossroad*

Edgar lives on welfare in a one-room, basement apartment. One afternoon the sheriff carried out an eviction order on the property of Ken, his neighbor. It was placed on the sidewalk in front of his home. Ken was in prison for shoplifting when this happened. Many people, walking past, helped themselves to Ken's belongings. Soon most of his good things were gone. Little remained for Ken after he was released from prison.

After Edgar saw what happened, he bought a bed, chair, and clothing from the Salvation Army for Ken. When he came home, Edgar found Ken an apartment and paid his first month's rent so that he could begin a new life. When the pastoral minister at St. Elizabeth's Church asked Edgar why he went out of his way to help Ken, he said, "Did not Jesus tell us that whatever we do for the least of our brothers and sisters, we do for him?" Faith-filled parishes are made up of people like Edgar.

In varied ways, parishes strive to meet people's spiritual and temporal needs. As parishes move into a new era, they are invited to build on the faith of parishioners like Edith and those who went before them. Parish ministers gain wisdom by examining how past generations of Catholics responded to the spiritual need of their times. They can better appreciate core Catholic beliefs and practices by examining the history of U.S. parishes. In so doing, it becomes apparent that whenever parishes faced significant changes, they adapted Jesus' unchanging message to the needs of their parishioners. This chapter examines changing parish life in four parts: Parishes—The Way They Were; Changes in Society, Changes in Parishes; Historical Crossroads in U.S. Parishes; Home Parishes: Early Catholic in America; and Pastoral Suggestions.

## Parishes—The Way They Were

When I was a boy, my life centered on our family and St. William's parish. We lived directly across the street from the church. Most people living in Price Hill, a suburb of Cincinnati, were Catholic. I only knew one Protestant, who lived down the street.

When I went outside my neighborhood to play sports, attend social events, or begin high school, I was often asked the question, "Where are you from?" I answered, "I am from St. William's Parish." Those hearing my response knew what I meant. Most of them were Catholic and answered saying, "I am from St. Lawrence, Holy Family, or St Theresa Parish."

We maintained a fierce loyalty to our parish. We were Catholics from St. William's and had little to do with the small Protestant church in our neighborhood, for we were forbidden to attend their worship services. Our loyalty to the Catholic Church was so strong that we sometimes wondered if it was okay to walk through their property. If we did, we'd get out of there as soon as possible.

We worked at our parish bingo and the summer festival. During warm evenings, neighbors watched as high school students gathered in St. William's schoolyard to play baseball. When it grew too dark to play ball, we sat on the school steps, talked, played cards, or arranged a game of "capture the flag." We knew the priests and sisters well and were delighted when they watched our games.

The same young people who came nightly to play ball often attended Mass each morning. During my high school years, as many as fifty high school students attended one of the six daily Masses in our parish before walking a mile or more to their respective high school.

Our lives centered on the parish. Everyone attended Mass on Sundays and holy days. We abstained from meat on Fridays and observed the Church's rules and regulations. The parish solidified our Catholic identity.

My experience at St. William's was not unique. In varying degrees, most Catholic parishioners reflected a similar loyalty and commitment. The parish was the spiritual, emotional, and physical focus of Catholic life. It offered a deep interior identity that gave us confidence. If something went wrong, our parish priests comforted us in our weakness, absolved our sins in confession, and gave us new hope. Early parish roots were deep and firm. When we left the parish and our lives took different paths, our Catholic identity, given us from our families and St. William's Parish, made us who we were.

## Changes in Society, Changes in Parishes

As society changed in the 1960s, the Catholic Church updated, and Vatican II moved it in new directions. These filtered into parishes, changing them from relatively stable, closed sociological units to more open communities of believers. Parishes entered into dialogue with Protestant and Jewish communities, used English in the liturgy, and engaged in social and civic enterprises unknown before the council. These changes brought shifts in Catholic belief and practice and clouded Catholic identity.

The changes in society and Church also affected the form and content of parish ministry. The 1983 *Code of Canon Law* describes the parish as "...a definite community of the Christian faithful, established on a stable basis within a particular church..." (canon 515, §1) The 1983 *Code* shifts the focus of the 1917 *Code* from a geographical one to a community of the faithful who share a common faith tradition. This faith tradition calls each parishioner to discipleship.

The parish teaches, deepens, and celebrates this call to discipleship. It reminds parishioners of Jesus' invitation to "follow him" and brings these words alive in their minds and hearts. In so doing, parishes help us discover the meaning of Jesus' good news, which centers on the kingdom of God.

From the beginning of the Christian era, Jesus' disciples gathered together to learn his message and celebrate it. Over the centuries such gatherings took different forms, one of which is the parish, which lives, proclaims, celebrates, and enfleshes God's kingdom.

How this occurs varies from parish to parish. It depends on pastoral leadership, community needs, and cultural conditions. Effective parishes recognize the inevitability of change and respond accordingly. This response meshes with an awareness of God as a god of love, not fear, and of Jesus as the God-man, not a divine unapproachable savior. Such an orientation affects theology, spirituality, and pastoral practice. It is influenced by parish leaders, community vitality, and the response to people's needs. This is illustrated in the following episode.

Father Jim has walked through the neighborhood daily in St. Barbara's parish from the time he arrived there ten years ago. He walks to the post office, business district, and grocery store. Sometimes he meets former parishioners. In conversations with them Father Jim discovered that some still live within the parish but transferred membership to another Catholic parish, joined a Protestant congregation, or dropped out. Since he was not the pastor when they attended St. Barbara's, former parishioners spoke more freely with him about why they left. He often found out that they left because the parish did not meet their or their children's needs, or church services were dull and uninspiring. Some people mentioned poor catechesis, liturgy, and preaching. Others said they no longer felt social pressure to go to Mass or belong to the parish. Still others described ministerial insensitivity that happened at traumatic moments, such as when they needed support and comfort. Such times may have included a family member's death, divorce, or serious sickness. As a part of the Catholic community, these parishioners had hoped for compassion and welcome. Because they did not find it, they left.

Some of these disillusioned parishioners had gravitated toward Catholic magnet parishes, so named because they attract parishioners from beyond their territorial boundaries with their quality of life, hospitality, catechesis, and worship. Most cities have one or more of these parishes. They affirm, nurture, and encourage people's desire for spiritual nourishment, wholeness, personal relationships, service, and global awareness.

As the above story indicates, Catholic parishes no longer maintain automatic loyalty from parishioners. In a recent publication a successful Protestant pastor advised newly formed churches that the most fertile source of new members was in the ranks of nonpracticing Catholics.

Many Catholics, but especially young adults, move toward emerging, loosely structured Christian churches that concentrate on hospitality, Bible readings, lively music, good preaching, and a casual atmosphere. One of these churches was formed after a business-executive-turned-pastor and several young associates conducted a market study of their area to ascertain people's needs and wants. After compiling the results they used the conclusions of their research to establish their church's orientation, structure, location, and style. This assembly is packed each Sunday. Many members are former Catholics.

Simply because Sunday Masses are filled, a parish has no reason to conclude that parishioners' spiritual needs are being met. To be a font of spiritual nourishment for contemporary Catholics, parishes need to be open to the changing needs of parishioners.

## Historical Crossroads in U.S. Parishes

When we look to the future of Catholic parishes, wisdom can be gained from our past history, which helps us appreciate the "crossroad" that Catholic parishes now face. Several times before, our parishes have experienced important crossroads. In analyzing them, it becomes clear that no single model of parish life suffices. Wherever parishes sprung up, they accommodated themselves to people's needs. Since our country's founding, Catholic life and practice has changed numerous times. As this happened, parishes also changed. The following statistics, based largely on *Catholicism USA* by Bryan T. Froehle and Mary L. Gautier, dramatically show this.

## *Home Parishes: Early Catholics in America*

Most early Catholics settled in Pennsylvania and Maryland. About 25,000 Catholics lived in this country when our Declaration of Independence was signed in 1776. At that time most Catholics lived on the East Coast. This minority population was generally looked down upon or persecuted. In 1800, Baltimore was the only diocese in the United States. There were thirty-five parishes to serve 35,000 Catholics throughout this country. Catholics were 1 percent of the population.

As Catholics moved away from the East Coast, some of them settled in the South, including in Florida, Louisiana, and along the southern Coast. Missionaries came through the northern states, especially the Great Lakes region. As this was happening, missionaries established missions in California, Texas, Arizona, and the Western states. In each instance the Catholic population gathered in faith communities to praise and worship God.

Early settlers in western areas took their Catholic faith with them as they came down the Ohio River in flatboats or over the Appalachian Mountains. Circuit-riding priests ministered to Catholic's spiritual needs while the family was the focus of their faith. Small prayer books often were given to families, especially to mothers, to teach Catholic belief and practice to their children.

During this early period, religious instruction, devotions, and worship centered in Catholic homes, for Catholics were few in numbers. Gradually, many changes occurred as catechesis and liturgy shifted from home to parish.

## Congregational Parishes: A Slow Emergence

Near the end of the eighteenth century and through the nineteenth century, the Catholic population increased. By 1850, the number of Catholics in the United States grew to over 1,600,000. This was 8 percent of the population. There were 1,073 parishes. Prior to 1850, parishes often had no resident pastor. Lay Catholics led these priestless parishes.

Lay trustees, who arranged for pastors to minister to the Catholic community, guided some parishes. These trustees continued their ministry even after resident pastors arrived. With few priests, Catholic faith, devotions, and religious instruction still centered in the home. Congregational parishes reached a "crossroad" in the mid-nineteenth century, when more priests arrived from Europe to assume parish leadership.

## Devotional Parishes: Growth and Solidification

Near the end of the nineteenth century, priests directed most parishes. Organizations developed, devotions were instituted, and Catholic life became solidified within the parish. Resident pastors refocused parishes in more organizational, hierarchical models as immigrants came from Ireland, Germany, Italy, Poland, and Eastern European countries. By 1900, the Catholic population rose to over 10 million. This was 14 percent of the population. There were 6,409 parishes.

As parishes became more clerical, Catholic belief and practice shifted from home to parish. Parishes grew in size, buoyed up by the deep faith of immigrant Catholics. The parish was the center of religious instruction, devotional life, and social activities. Men's and women's societies, children and youth programs, Catholic schools, parish religious instructions, sacraments, Mass, and devotions addressed Catholic needs.

These devotional parishes established the groundwork for strong pre–Vatican II parishes like St. William's. They were characterized by clericalism and an emphasis on the Mass, Rosary, devotions, sin, and confession.

## Freely Chosen Parishes

By 1950, the Catholic population grew to over 26 million, which was 19 percent of the population. There were 15,553 parishes. As Catholics increased in numbers, another crossroad occurred in U.S. parishes. This happened in the 1960s, as a result of cultural and societal changes and the shifts in the Church after Vatican II.

Following the council, changes came rapidly in church architecture, liturgy, religious education, social involvement, and the configuration of parish ministries. These changes confused many parishioners who were not prepared for them. Many Catholics did not understand the "what, why, and who" of these changes.

Parishes responded to the directives of the council, and lay participation and new programs developed. Such changes put a heavy stress on pastors and church ministers. Coupled with new pastoral directives, parishes sensed growing demands from African American, Vietnamese, Asian, Hispanic, and other ethnic Catholics. Such demands led them to refocus parish music and religious perspectives to celebrate the ethnic heritage of new parishioners. At the same time, women became more sensitive to their place in the church, the permanent diaconate started, religious communities updated, lay ministries grew, and clerical numbers dropped.

This climate brought about changing responsibilities, shifts in catechetical and liturgical practices, multiple committees, meetings, and financial considerations. Many parishes employed business models and practices to address such changes, which brought more complex church structures and budgets. These sometimes clouded the parish's mission of proclaiming Jesus' message. Such uncertainty, coupled with increasing secular demands, made effective parish ministry challenging.

Today, Catholic parishes have stabilized. Lay ministry grows, priestly identity clarifies, catechesis and liturgy improve, and adult faith formation programs and biblical studies have taken hold. Women now play a major role in parish ministry, taking graduate ministerial degrees or being involved in ministry formation programs. A high percentage of parish ministers, serving various functions, are women. On a diocesan level, women serve as canon lawyers and in other staff ministries. Church ministry often flourishes because of them. Without dedicated, faith-filled women, the Church could not adequately function.

In addition to the explosion of lay ministers serving parishes, particularly the contributions of women, another positive sign of the parish's vitality is the service provided by permanent deacons. Many of them work in parish sacramental and service ministries. They assist at the liturgy, catechize, coordinate parish programs, visit the sick, and administer parishes. Diaconal ministry enriches parishes and serves as a model for the Catholic laity.

These developments since Vatican II put parishes at another crossroad. At the beginning of the second millennium, Catholics numbered over 59 million which was around 22 percent of the total population. There were about 19,000 parishes.

A hopeful vision of tomorrow's parish accepts the challenges facing the Church. These are unlike those previously experienced in U.S. Catholic history and put U.S. parishes at a new threshold. Identifying them enables parishes to see where they are strong and where they need to change.

## Pastoral Suggestions

An analysis of key dimensions of yesterday's parish helps us consider the challenges of today. Taking our point of departure from the materials discussed in this chapter, the following suggestions are offered for parishes:

- Ask several senior members of the parish to arrange a session for parishioners that identifies key changes in parish life during the past thirty years.

- Appoint an ad hoc committee to identify the social conditions that impact upon the parish's identity, needs, mission, and ministry.

- Ask parishioners to fill out a questionnaire to be dropped in the collection basket, inquiring how the parish is fulfilling their needs.

- Set aside ten minutes at each parish council meeting for specific ministries to explain how they stress welcome and hospitality.

- Reach out to strangers and neighbors, asking parishioners to invite a guest to a special Sunday event in the spring and fall.

- Survey parishioners yearly to ascertain how their catechetical and liturgical needs are met.

- Have a parish volunteer look into the various options available for social ministry in the neighborhood and put these options on the parish Web site.

- Encourage alienated Catholics to return to the parish by initiating some form of a "Come Back Home" program for inactive Catholics.

- Ask the parish council to conduct a yearly evaluation of the parish's management system.

- Plan a celebration to invite parishioners to learn more about the parish's history, including the neighborhood and ethnic people who founded it.

Parishes are in a position to make a difference in society by facing the reality of the times and developing the spirituality of parish members. In so doing, parishes follow in the footsteps of those who preceded them by bringing Jesus' message of hope to the twenty-first century.

## 2.

# *Facing the New Crossroad*

Old Eddie lived alone. He had no relatives and a small pension. Each Sunday, two parishioners from St. Bernard's parish picked him up and brought him to Mass. Father Chas looked forward to seeing Eddie's joyful face when the priest came to the back of church before beginning the liturgy. So did the rest of the parishioners. Eddie was an informal greeter standing each Sunday in the vestibule supported by his cane. His arthritic hands stretched out to welcome anyone who stopped to say, "Good Morning."

One Christmas season, Father Chas told Eddie he liked his new coat. The old man smiled and said, "Do you really think it's new? I bought it fifty years ago." On another occasion, the priest asked him how the parishioners treat him. Eddie replied, "Great, Father! From Tuesday on each week I look forward to Sunday when I come to church. It is the best part of my week." Eddie was usually the first person at Mass and the last one to leave.

When Eddie died, the same parishioners who brought him to Mass took care of his funeral arrangements. After the Mass of Christian Burial, they distributed his few earthly possessions. When they came to close up his apartment, they discovered everything in order. They gave his old, but clean clothes and the rest of the apartment contents to the St. Vincent de Paul thrift store. They left with an old cigar box containing some cuff links, a few medals, and $5.38, all that remained of Eddie's life and possessions. They knew, however, that much more remained. Eddie died as he lived—a happy man, leaving his legacy of care, joy, and happiness in the hearts of the parishioners who were his family.

Parishes play a vital role in the lives of many Catholics like Eddie. As *Our Hearts Were Burning Within Us* says, "For most Catholics, the parish is their primary experience of the Church. It is where they gather for weekly worship, celebrate their most joyous occasions, and mourn their deepest losses" (p. 40). Parishes are a vital part of Catholic life. This chapter invites parishes to face the new crossroad, as they proclaim Jesus' message and meet people's spiritual needs. It does so in four parts, namely, Shifting Theological and Pastoral Perspectives, Facing the New Crossroad, Internal Dynamics Facing Parish Life, and Pastoral Suggestions.

## Shifting Theological and Pastoral Perspectives

The Second Vatican Council shifted the theology underlying parish life. The *Dogmatic Constitution on the Church (Lumen Gentium)* focused on the Church as the people of God. This orientation led to significant changes in parish ministry and organizational structures and transformed the responsibilities of parish members. Ministry, once the domain of ordained clergy, was now framed within the baptismal call of all Christians.

After the council, changes occurred in religious education, liturgy, religious garb, laws of fast and abstinence, and lay involvement in parish life. Catholics were encouraged to address the problems of society. Increasingly, the laity became involved in liturgical, catechetical, and social ministries. Some Catholics accepted these changes enthusiastically, while others did not.

Rather than enhance Catholic confidence, such changes often brought uncertainty and confusion. The unrest that was sweeping through society as a whole entered Catholic seminaries and universities in the late 1960s. Yet energy was high, and many believed that the optimism they experienced would last indefinitely. What happened in Catholic circles mirrored the unrest in secular society where civil rights protests, Woodstock, the Kent State shootings, and Vietnam took center stage.

During the 1970s and 1980s new ministries sprung up in parishes. They focused on religious education, liturgical renewal, social concerns, separated and divorced Catholics, family ministry, the Rite of Christian Initiation of Adults (RCIA), and youth ministry. Lay men and women became readers, eucharistic ministers, and cantors. Directors of religious education were hired to deal with new challenges in catechetical ministry. As parish staffs grew in size, tensions sometimes arose between ministries, including the parish school of religion and the Catholic school. Such tensions often involved competition for a share of the parish's financial pie.

By the 1990s the ministry explosion was in full swing. The Catholic laity served in a variety of ways. As liturgy and catechesis improved, the uncertainties of the previous twenty years subsided. Parishes stood at a new crossroad. This was energized by the success of the Rite of Christian Initiation of Adults and the publication of the *Catechism of the Catholic Church*. The former symbolizes the Church's present dynamism; the latter symbolizes the growing stability in the Catholic community.

Today, parish ministry continues to increase in quality and completeness. Theological and pastoral directions initiated by Vatican II are now in place. At this new crossroad, great things are happening in many parishes. Spiritual, social, educational, liturgical, and service ministries abound. Parish ministers are well educated, often having a master's degree or a doctorate.

St. Casmir Parish, located in a large mid-Western city, publishes a fifteen-page bulletin each week with information on social activities and parish ministries. It describes opportunities for spiritual direction, counseling, and homebound ministry. It advertises sessions for catechesis on all levels, sacramental preparation programs, Emmaus ministry, MOMS (Ministry of Mothers Sharing) ministry, Moms in Prayer, Boy Scouts, Girl Scouts, annulment seminars, and parenting skills for the separated and divorced. The bulletin announces a "Meet Jesus Again" seminar, an invitation to "share your Advent and Christmas traditions," a celebration of World Youth Day, social ministries, and Friends of Children with Special Needs Support Groups. It offers volunteer opportunities for seniors, job fairs, a meeting of unemployed parishioners helping each other, Yaach Club (young adults in their 20s–30s) announcements, depression discussions, weekly Web pages, and Respect Life programs. This parish stresses hospitality. One result is that it has over seventy converts in the RCIA each year. When seeing this parish and others like it in action, it becomes clear that great things are happening in many parishes. Whether large or small, they serve as models and portend even greater future blessings.

## Facing the New Crossroad

The crossroad at which today's parishes find themselves offers many challenges, as parishes bring their mission and ministry to the modern world. While these are formidable, the hope and enthusiasm in our parishes provides confidence that future parishes will be strong. This strength arises from the belief that most parishes provide opportunities for spiritual growth, scripture studies, solid catechesis, vibrant liturgies, and outreach to the poor. It also comes out of people's realization of their baptismal call and mandate to minister in the world.

As parish staffs grow in confidence and the Catholic laity serve various ministries in unprecedented numbers, Catholic pride grows. This increases when parishioners participate in welcoming the stranger and creating a more humane, loving society. In this regard, the book *Sons and Daughters of the Light: A Pastoral Plan for Ministry with Young Adults* says, "Many young adults are willing to share their leadership skills in ministry and their deep spirituality with their new parish community" (p. 2). Future parish vitality will depend on how parishes welcome and encourage young adults. Parishes can take their cue from the zeal that young people show in volunteering for projects like Habitat for Humanity and service ministries after they graduate from college.

What is occurring in parishes portends a new explosion of God's word. This demands openness to change and commitment to Catholic values. A parish's task is to prepare parishioners, especially youth, to become citizens of the world. Catholic social teaching encourages parishes to educate its members to see people of various races and nationalities as brothers and sisters. This means developing attitudes in children, youth, and adults that respect all cultures and religions while maintaining loyalty to the Catholic faith. It means knowing the basic teachings and practices of the Catholic faith and being comfortable enough to share them with others. It involves a strong commitment to solid catechesis on all levels focusing on adult faith formation.

As the Church enters into dialogue with world cultures and religions, it takes steady steps toward inculturation. This has practical implications for the parish as more people of non-Christian religions like Buddhists, Muslims, and Hindus enter our parish boundaries, work in our offices and factories, and attend school with our children. This was illustrated in the remarks of Father Gary, who described what happened after he preached a homily on the scripture readings in light of *Jesus the Lord,* a document treating the relationship between Jesus, the Catholic Church, other Christian denominations, and world religions. To make his point about God's presence in religions or denominations beyond the Catholic Church, Father Gary quoted the *Dogmatic Constitution on the Church* from Vatican II, the foundation for interpreting subsequent writings on this subject.

After Mass, a woman told him, "I have never been as proud of my Catholic faith as today because I now understand the reasons why the Church teaches what it does and how the Church respects other religious beliefs." With eyes beaming, she described the significance of informing the Catholic laity on current Church issues to inflame their zeal in proclaiming Jesus' message. While she spoke, a teenage girl and her grandmother listened. The older woman said, "When you gave your homily, my granddaughter, Sally, clapped her hands under the pew and whispered to me, 'Amen! Right on!'" This high school girl has Buddhist and Muslim friends. While recognizing the distinctiveness of her Catholic faith, Sally wanted to hear from her pastor that God walks with good people of all religions. As Father Gary was about to leave them, Sally asserted her pride as she volunteered to be a reader at Mass.

Parishioners learn the latest Catholic developments from newspapers, television, and the Internet. They need the Church to help them sort out conflicting perspectives. That's why pastoral sessions, like those described above in St. Casmir's bulletin, are so important. Parishes help people when they connect Catholic doctrine and moral belief with issues that interest them, instead of regulating current affairs to a side shelf.

While challenges lie ahead, the emerging Catholic spirit makes the Church confident that parishes will be stronger than ever. The Holy Spirit is active in parishioners' hearts as they seek deeper spirituality and better ways to minister in their families, neighborhoods, and parishes.

## Internal Dynamics Facing Parish Life

Changes in U.S. parishes during the past two hundred years are a prelude to the challenges now facing the Church. Regardless of the future, Catholics need a stable core of faith that sociological, demographic, ethnic, personnel, or family changes cannot influence. Such stability comes from Jesus Christ, who grounds our lives and ministry. Life with Jesus centers on love of God and neighbor, as reflected in the words of *Our Hearts Were Burning Within Us*: "Christian faith is lived in discipleship to Jesus Christ" (p. 15). This involves acting justly and morally in a world that hungers for meaning. Such stability invites parishes to refocus their ministry on parishioners' spiritual needs, to examine challenges to its life, confident that the risen Lord is leading them into a vibrant future.

As a result of Vatican II, parish dynamics shifted. The *Pastoral Constitution on the Church in the Modern World (Gaudium et Spes)* challenges Catholics to influence the world by their presence, for society is a fertile ground for Christian discipleship. Catholics living in a pluralistic society are invited to reach out to the broader culture through ecumenism and social involvement. As this happens, cultural values influence parishes. Advances in science, technology, food production, and medicine afford parishes new opportunities to help parishioners appreciate their calling to use these resources to develop a better, healthier world.

At the same time, cultural relativism, materialism and individualism can easily distract parishioners from core life issues. The Church cannot protect Catholics from the temptations of secular society, as unknown challenges confront them in their homes, work, and parish. It can, however, give them direction on how to face them. While secular challenges are formidable, many Church issues are equally challenging. These challenges, coming from a variety of sources, include the following.

## Ethnic Diversity

About fifteen Hispanic Catholics attend St. George's Parish each Sunday at the 11:00 a.m. Mass and their numbers increase steadily. They always sit in the last pews of church. One Sunday, a parish minister asked if any parishioner ever welcomed them or asked them to get involved in parish ministry. The father of a family said, "Except for the pastor, who always welcomes us when we enter church, no one else ever greets us." He continued, "It's not that we feel shunned. If one of us says 'hello' to someone at church, we get a nice reply. It would be appreciated, however, if a parishioner asked us our names or where we live. After all, the parish is not that big. When one of my children stopped in the Protestant church up the block, she was asked to join the youth club the first time she attended. In our previous Catholic parish, we felt at home. This has not happened here."

The episode illustrates the importance of raising awareness of the important role parishioners play in welcoming new people. It also points out the shifting ethnic configurations that challenge a parish. Such changes offer many opportunities to enrich liturgy, catechesis, and pastoral ministry by drawing from the rich cultural heritage that ethnic groups bring.

Most parishes have Hispanic, African American, Near Eastern, or Asian parishioners. How parishes respond to such diversity affects whether the parish benefits from their cultural gifts and whether people of various ethnic backgrounds become active parishioners. Often, parish responses occur gradually, but none succeed without a commitment of parishioners to hospitality. With such a commitment, multi-ethnic songs, catechesis, festivals, foods, and customs can be introduced. Food festivals, sponsored by different ethnic groups, may be the first step toward other events stressing different cultural dimensions, like ethnic Christmas celebrations, music, and clothing.

In *Unity and Diversity: Welcoming the Stranger Among Us,* the U.S. bishops address the issue of the immigrants in our country. They stress welcoming and respecting their cultures. In a section on the parish, they say, "Immigrants will experience the Church's welcome most personally at the level of the parish. Pastors and pastoral staffs, accordingly, must be filled with a spirit of welcome, responding to a new and perhaps little-understood culture" (p. 43).

## Various Family Configurations

In a Catholic elementary school, a fifth-grade teacher was surprised when a child told her that visiting her grandparents was no big thing because she had eight grandparents. Both her parents were divorced and remarried. Another child said he did not know three of his grandparents, and the fourth lives two thousand miles away. More and more children do not live with their parents.

Family diversity continues to increase. Effective pastoral ministers cannot presume that children seeking religious instruction, first communion, or confirmation come from a household of father, mother, and children. Some of them live in blended or divorced families. Some live with grandparents or other family configurations. Many households may not have a Catholic orientation. Even in Catholic homes, pastoral ministers cannot conclude that children pray, learn about God, attend Mass, and receive the sacraments.

On the other hand, most parents, whatever the family background, try to provide their children with a good home, clothing, education, and religious upbringing. Sometimes they do this at great personal sacrifice.

God's special gifts are found in every home, regardless of its size or shape. Pastoral ministers can help parents and heads of households acknowledge their gifts and respond to them in the spirit of Christ. As the *General Directory for Catechesis* says, "…The Christian community must give very special attention to parents. By means of personal contact, meetings, courses and also adult catechesis directed toward parents, the Christian community must help them assume their responsibility—which is particularly delicate today—of educating their children in the faith" (#227).

## The Priest Shortage

The priest shortage in the United States is serious. Many parishes are changing because of it, others are closing. The priest shortage accelerates the need to prepare more lay administrators, permanent deacons, and pastoral ministers.

Few previous generations have witnessed lay Catholics taking such important roles in Church leadership. These lay Catholics serve out of a deep conviction that the Lord invites them to minister in the Church community as a response to their baptismal calling. Because of the priest shortage, Catholics parishes are learning new ways to be "Church."

The priest shortage has brought many challenges. In large parishes with only a pastor, his work can be overwhelming. Many priests may pastor three or four parishes. This adds to the physical and emotional burdens of an aging clergy. Some bishops use priests from other countries, who often do not understand U.S. culture and whose English is difficult for Americans to understand. Some parishes without resident pastors substitute a communion service for Sunday Mass. If continued for long, this practice brings negative consequences, for the Catholic Church builds its theology and pastoral practice around the Mass. How do children, growing up without the regular celebration of the Eucharist, appreciate the fullness of the Catholic faith? The declining number of ordained priests available for parish ministry is refocusing the way parish ministry happens.

The decreasing number of priests has resulted in closing or consolidating parishes. Wherever this happens, it brings pain and disillusionment to Catholics who took pride in their former parish. Because of the strong bonding associated with belonging to a parish, closing a parish often is not the best option. This has particular impact in rural areas where parishes are scattered many miles apart. Many of these small churches were begun by the Catholic laity who asked a priest to serve in their parish.

A mid-West parish, founded in the nineteenth century, began when visiting priests celebrated the Eucharist and solemnized marriages several times a year in a church built by the laity. If a priest was not available for a long time, a revered parish member baptized the children. It is paradoxical that some parishes like this are now being closed because there are no priests.

Dioceses are looking for ways to keep parishes open and to minister in such situations, and options are being explored, including various configurations of pastors and pastoral administrators. Rather than closing such parishes, is it not worth considering hiring pastoral administrators to coordinate the ministries of Word, worship, and service, and to arrange for a priest to periodically celebrate the Eucharist, sacrament of healing and reconciliation? Closing a parish without serious consultation with parishioners often has devastating results. Several years ago, a small rural parish was closed by the diocese in spite of parishioner protests. Unknown to those outside the area, when the church was sold, a parish representative bought it. A non-Catholic minister was hired, and most parishioners joined the new congregation now housed in their old church. Even the name remained the same, but it was no longer a Catholic church.

Many dioceses arrange parishes in clusters and assign a pastor to several parishes. Full or part-time ministers of administration and service, as well as permanent deacons, complement his ministry. Each of these parishes functions as a parish even if the pastor's time or energy does not permit him to celebrate Mass every Sunday in every one.

Many pastors serve two or more parishes. Since each situation is different, no fixed norms can be given for the best model to adopt. It is important, however, that Mass be celebrated on a regular basis, even if not weekly, in each parish. In addition, parishioners' other spiritual needs have to be met. The goal of any effort to reorganize parish configurations is to serve the people, keep parishes open, and help priests avoid burnout. In dealing with the priest shortage, it is clear that the health of priests is an important factor to consider in future decisions.

Parish closings may be the most viable option when socioeconomic conditions have shifted the demographics of a city or rural area. In such cases, it is important to consult parishioners for their advice and to respect their feelings. Ideally, they ought to be the ones who decide with help from the diocese about the parish's future. When a parish is closed, parishioners need to feel they have been heard.

Each parish is unique and is to be treated as such, especially when faced with consolidation or closing. Geography, ethnic diversity, and socioeconomic factors play significant roles in discerning what to do. The following guidelines are suggested when consolidating or closing a parish is an issue:

- The priest shortage alone cannot be the prime factor driving parish closings.

- If no other major obstacles exist (financial, demographic), beyond the absence of a priest, the parish usually ought to remain open.

- Any decisions about a parish's future are made with serious consultation of the parishioners.

- An overall plan for pastoral ministry is established on a geographical basis, sometimes on a deanery basis, when information is available about the number of priests that the area can expect in the future.

- Such a plan provides for continued catechetical, sacramental, and service ministries when parishes have no full-time ministers.

- In parish closings, great sensitivity is given to the parishioners, lest they leave and join another

Christian community. For many Catholics, Eucharist and community are vital. When a parish is closed, some Catholics may leave the Church if these factors are not addressed. This happened in one African American inner-city parish that was consolidated with two other Catholic parishes. Many parishioners were converts to the Catholic Church from the Baptist religion. They felt strong support from their Catholic parish. When it was closed, they did not go to the new parish some distance away, where they felt little community. Instead, they returned to their former Baptist congregation.

- In parishes without adequate ministers, a parish administrator, associate, or coordinator, working in close conjunction with the diocese and deanery, sees that the parishioners' spiritual needs are met. This includes coordinating some ministries with neighboring parishes.

- Each parish establishes its own ministerial plan with the guidelines established by the diocese.

Father Jake, a pastor who served rural parishes for many years, commented perceptively on the challenge afforded when parish consolidation is the issue. He says, "Often, full-time salaries over and beyond the pastor's are not available. It may take time for parishioners to respect 'one of their own' as their leader rather than the priest. For this reason, lay leadership training is essential. The clergy, too, may need retooling to acquire the skills necessary to share leadership roles with the laity."

Many priests in rural parishes spend considerable time with parishioners whom they know personally. Father Jake continues, "It will be hard for such priests to become primarily circuit-riding, sacramental ministers. I am not accustomed to marrying and burying people that I do not know. I am not happy about the prospect of either becoming the norm. The informality of rural parishes requires the meshing of the priest's and parishioners' personalities. The wrong priest in a small parish can quickly have devastating results."

## Economic Diversity of Parishioners

Emily met Tosha while the latter bagged groceries at the local market. Emily noticed her heavy accent and learned she was a recent immigrant to the United States. Tosha said that she wanted to take English courses to find a better job to support her family who lived near the poverty level. Embarrassed to let anyone know they needed help, Tosha shied away from going to church for she could not provide new clothing for her family.

Emily enjoyed prosperity while Tosha struggled. Such people often sit side by side in church every Sunday, unaware of each other's plight. As the social and economic disparity between rich and poor Catholics grows, parishes are challenged to minister to all parishioners regardless of their economic condition. To do this, parishes can make funds available to help the needy and develop ways to link parishioners without jobs with those who can help them. Parish volunteers can assist people to prepare resumes and be a clearinghouse for agencies that offer training in English and job placement. The social sector contains opportunities for free services that many needy parishioners do not realize are available.

The ethnic, social, and economic disparity of Catholics presents formidable ministerial challenges. Although it is often easier to minister to those who speak the English language and understand American customs, Jesus' message challenges parishes to recognize every person's equality before God.

## Emerging Role of the Laity

A parish ministry fair provides a practical way to invite the laity to learn different ways to serve. People who get involved in parish ministry often grow in their faith. Many Protestant churches require volunteer service as a condition of joining the church. Such a commitment helps new members recognize the responsibility of their baptismal commitment.

As the Catholic laity respond to the Spirit's call to offer their gifts, parishes have refocused old ministries and developed new ways to serve. Stewardship includes giving one's time, talent, and treasure. While money (treasure) is necessary in any parish, it is equally important to stress time and talent. Stewardship Sunday provides an opportunity to energize parish educational efforts from childhood to old age.

To enhance the role of lay ministry, parish leaders need to plan new ministries, support existing ones, and intervene when opposition surfaces, jealousies arise, or unhealthy politics occur. Sometimes conflicts arise from the unbending conviction of individuals or pressure groups. Such conflicts need to be resolved for effective parish ministry to happen.

## Lay Spirituality

Sensitive parish ministers recognize people's spiritual hunger and consider new avenues for spiritual renewal. This was illustrated when two women asked me to help them develop scripture courses on a regional level. Soon two other women joined the group. We began an Adult Spirituality Institute, which is well organized and taught by outstanding professors. The key to the Institute's success is the quality of the teachers who apply biblical research, spirituality, and faith to the participant's real-life situations.

Previously, the Church honed the spirituality of priests, brothers, and sisters. Today, a new tradition of Catholic lay spirituality is developing. It includes spiritual direction, scripture studies, the lives of the saints, prayer opportunities, days of recollection, and directed retreats for parishioners of various ages, ethnic backgrounds, and social and economic conditions. *The Vocation and the Mission of the Lay Faithful in the Church and the World* says, "The fundamental objective of the formation of the lay faithful is an ever-clearer discovery of one's vocation and the ever-greater willingness to live it so as to fulfil one's mission" (#58).

Parishes are invited to center their ministries on adult faith formation. Some parishes hire a spiritual director to facilitate lay spirituality, teach spiritual companioning skills, and offer spiritual counseling. Spiritual companioning means that one lay person walks with someone else as a trusted, spiritual friend in good and difficult times. It involves informal spiritual direction.

More than a faith-filled, vibrant, prayerful Sunday liturgy is needed to meet people's spiritual needs. They hunger for deeper connections with God and ways to help them grow spiritually in their everyday lives. The traditions of Catholic devotional life, common before Vatican II, need to be refocused in light of the developments since the council. A parish must minister spiritually to adults by responding as Jesus did when the disciples asked him, "Lord, teach us to pray."

## Pastoral Leadership

Father Bill, pastor of a midsized parish, struggled each Sunday with his homily. He was a quiet administrator. People who knew him superficially might not have seen him as an outstanding leader. For those who knew him well, however, it was different. Father Bill usually was around the parish center and school rectory when he was not visiting parishioners, walking around the neighborhood, or assisting the sick and dying. He regularly went into the classrooms and helped with the parish school religion program. He also visited the local shopkeepers and listened to those needing counseling.

Father Bill developed a serious sickness and died two years later. In planning the funeral, parish leaders decided that the grade-school children would not attend except for representatives of the upper classes. The rest of the children complained when they learned of this decision. Child after child said, "Father Bill was my friend. He baptized me, gave me first communion, and visited my house. He played in the schoolyard. I want to be there." All the schoolchildren attended his funeral.

Father Bill's story illustrates that pastoral leadership involves using one's God-given gifts in the spirit of the gospels. No one model exists for successful parish leaders. A leader is in touch with people's needs and responds with the gifts that the Lord has given, using these gifts to inspire others to follow Jesus.

## Different Agendas and Demands

All parish decisions are intended to serve people's needs. Sometimes disagreements surface about parish priorities. These may involve, for example, tensions between an education commission and an athletic group that are arguing over money. It may be a turf conflict between liturgical and catechetical ministers. If handled right, these can become a source of blessing, for they present opportunities for educating parishioners on the implications of Jesus' message.

Parishioners have different priorities. These may involve whether the parish should place a higher stress on building a new church, serving the poor, entering a partnership (twinning) with an inner-city parish, strengthening the liturgy, or developing better children's religious formation and youth ministry programs. Such issues challenge a parish to sort out its priorities in light of Jesus' teachings.

## Various Faith Levels and Moral Perspectives

In surveying Catholic young adults, one minister reported the following results. Some respondents said they believed in God but made no commitment to Jesus or the Church. Others believed in God and Jesus but made no commitment to the Church. A minority made a commitment to God, Jesus, and the Church. Their responses indicate that their faith journeys differ. By presuming various faith levels, the Rite of Christian Initiation of Adults reminds parishes to provide different opportunities for people to walk their unique journeys with God. In so doing, they support the conversion process in people's lives. Such support is critical, for the faith level of active and inactive Catholics is different. Mass and the sacraments do not nourish all parishioners equally, and Catholics differ in their beliefs about Jesus' presence in the Eucharist and their attitude toward the sacrament of reconciliation. Effective parishes offer various options for different faith needs. These may include sessions for mothers, men's meetings, and programs for returning Catholics and for children of divorce.

Something similar exists with moral perspectives. Unlike previous generations, some Catholics give little regard to what the Church teaches is right and wrong on issues affecting their lives. Many Catholics say they accept basic Church teachings but disagree on issues like birth control, the morality of war, premarital sex, and capital punishment. It is important for ministers to address such moral issues in light of church teaching when teaching, preaching, and advising parishioners.

## Hunger for a Meaningful Community

Jesus provides the answer to the loneliness, fear, and ambiguity that affects many children, youth, married people, singles, and older adults. This generation hungers for relationships that go beyond functional activities. To find such relationships, some people join gangs or take drugs. Others substitute money, work, sports, and superficial relationships for the deeper ones they lack.

Tapping into this spiritual hunger and the need for meaningful relationships is a key to successful parish ministry. It provides an opportunity to minister to people who need to feel loved and a part of something. In a world where money is often more important than relationships, hospitable parishes provide a much-needed environment where relationships can develop. The importance of hospitality is evident in the story of Melissa, who went to a Protestant church to fulfill an assignment for her Catholic high school religion class. When she returned home, Melissa contrasted the Catholic Mass with this Protestant worship service. She said, "The welcome I experienced and the community I felt moved me to return to the Protestant church again even though I remain an active Catholic." Today, many people feel a similar welcome and community spirit when they enter Catholic parishes. Catholic hospitality is the first step to a fully revitalized parish, centered on Jesus.

## Pastoral Suggestions

The following pastoral suggestions arise from the considerations of this chapter:

- Ask the youth minister to survey the youth in the parish to ascertain their spiritual needs.
- Form an ad hoc committee of young people and adults to study why some teenagers do not attend parish religious instructions, youth groups, Mass, and the sacraments and to devise ways to welcome back to the parish those teens who have left.
- Invite the parish youth club or several young people to take charge of a particular parish ministry, like arranging a weekly or monthly prayer service for peace.
- Develop a process whereby the renewal of worship space impacts a parish positively rather than being a divisive element. In this regard, appoint a committee to study this issue, survey successes and failures in other parishes, and make specific recommendations.
- Invite a group of longtime parishioners to ask new parishioners of various ethnic backgrounds to help them come up with ways to welcome them and celebrate their ethnic cultures.
- Survey the parish to target inactive Catholics, ascertain why they left, and invite them back.

- Form a special committee to study programs available elsewhere that welcome back inactive Catholics. Have the committee look into which programs are successful and would best serve the parish, centered on Jesus.

- Invite volunteers from the business community to contact men and women in various professions, asking them to recommend ways for the parish to support parishioners in their work in the marketplace.

- Invite the social-action committee to consider new ways to discuss with neighboring churches cooperative ventures aimed at serving needy people.

- Form a men's group if one does not exist, to address the spiritual needs of men, considering possible men's ministries like Morning Prayer breakfasts, Saturday men's sharing groups, days of renewal, and retreats. The same can be done for women.

- Study the parish's altar server lists to ascertain whether, as more girls become altar servers, the boys lose interest or drop out. If this is the case, devise ways to address this issue.

- Have an outside consultant evaluate the parish's organizational structure to discover how well each organization and ministry, including pastoral or parish council and finance council, serves parishioners and reaches out in welcome to the wider community.

- After the above evaluation is complete, have the parish council recommend which organizations are to be continued, changed, merged, strengthened, or dropped.

- Do a yearly evaluation of the effectiveness of the professional staff, including how they work together, their contributions, strengths and tensions, and the justness of their salaries, benefits, and time expectations on their job.

- Plan for a staff day of reflection to examine parish meetings, professional updating, retreats, days of recollection, and other renewal processes, such as Renew, *koinoia,* and small faith communities.

- Ask the chairpersons of all the parish ministries to examine the parish's vision to ascertain how it is being met and if any changes are in order.

- Make available to interested parishioners a list of social agencies where they can volunteer their services.

- Ask the spiritual life committee to study the advantages of hiring a full or part-time spiritual counselor to enhance the spiritual life of the parish as a whole, deal with various specific ministries, and assist teachers and children in the Catholic school or parish school of religion.

The pastoral perspectives described in this chapter set the stage for looking more intently at people's needs, which will be addressed in Chapter Three.

# 3.

# *Centering on People's Needs*

Sara was dying in a nursing home. She turned critical on Sunday afternoon, and Mary, her daughter, called several churches to get a priest to anoint her. Mary found no one, so she and her brother drove to a neighboring parish. It was raining very hard as they approached the rectory. They saw a car coming out of the driveway. When the driver saw them, he stopped. They rolled down their window, and Mary said that her dying mother needed a priest. The man identified himself as Father Bill. He got the holy oils and they went to anoint Sara.

The time spent in the nursing home anointing Sara was beautiful and prayerful. Father Bill remained with the family long afterward and afforded consolation for Sara and her family. Later Mary called the parish and said that the support they received was a "God send"—just what they needed.

Parishes exist to help people grow spiritually and support them in difficult times. Catholics look for a welcoming parish that provides comfort, good religious education, spiritual programs, and liturgies. The *General Directory for Catechesis* sums up the parish's importance when it says, "The parish is, without doubt, the most important *locus* in which Christian community is formed and expressed. This is called to be a fraternal and welcoming family where Christians become aware of being the people of God" (#257, cf. 67c.).

People are attracted to a welcoming, supportive parish. This is especially important during transition periods such as birth, death, marriage, divorce, adolescence, young adulthood, and older age. Meeting people's needs begins with hospitality. St. Bede's parish had a strong resurgence of parishioners after Father Jeff became pastor. When asked what the secret to the parish's revitalization was, he said, "Hospitality! Hospitality! Hospitality! Hospitality! Everything we do is based on hospitality. When people feel welcome and wanted, all the other ministries flow."

A welcoming parish community lays the groundwork for addressing parishioners' needs. Without hospitality, ministerial efforts languish. This chapter looks at the following four points: Catholic Identity, Addressing Peoples' Needs, Recreating the Parish, and Pastoral Suggestions.

## Catholic Identity

Many questions surround Catholic identity, including the question, "What does it mean to be a Catholic?" There is a close relationship between identity and ritual patterns. Rituals establish an emotional bonding between people. This happens, for example, in the rituals of married life, which reflect ways that spouses express love, deal with difficulties, show forgiveness, and balance personal and work patterns. Rituals ground family expectations and afford the confidence to know what to expect in daily affairs. Something similar exists in larger groups like a parish. Church rituals establish a comfort zone for those who identify with them.

Identity is born from the interchange between rituals and emotional responses. Catholic rituals make us feel at home and comfortable with Catholic ways of acting. In childhood, my parents would inquire if there was a Catholic church in the area where we planned to vacation, before finalizing our plans. Attending Sunday Mass was part of our identity. During her lifetime, even at ninety-one years of age, if my mother could not get to Mass on a given Sunday, she would not go anywhere else on that day.

Rituals exercise four functions related to identity. First, they *establish identity* as we internalize group rituals. This happens with children raised in a Catholic home that practices the faith on a regular basis. It also occurs as the Church initiates catechumens into the faith through the Rite of Christian Initiation of Adults. Second, they *focus identity*. Catholic ritual patterns differ from those of Methodists or Buddhists. Such differences focus the identity patterns of each group. Third, rituals help us *redirect identity*. When a loved one dies, serious sickness happens, or a breadwinner loses a job, an identity disruption occurs. Ritual patterns of love and compassion from friends, family, and parishioners help people redirect their identity focus as they come to grips with changing life patterns. Finally, rituals *reestablish identity*. This may happen after a young adult leaves home for college and feels the loss of family and friends. In time, new friends and responsibilities help reestablish the student's identity. Something similar happens when a person loses a job then finds a new one or when someone who has lost a spouse chooses the single life or remarries.

The connection between ritual, emotional response, and identity affects people differently. The process of refocusing the Church's theological and pastoral orientation after Vatican II continues. This goes on as new ritual patterns reflecting Catholic core belief and practice emerge. Examples include the specification of the clergy's role, support for lay ministry, clarification of Church doctrine, and solidification of liturgical practices, especially the Rite of Christian Initiation of Adults. An illustration of identity clarification is the pride that many Catholics take in their parishes.

On a level deeper than rational analysis, the Catholic community is now clarifying what it means to be Catholic. Today, Catholic identity is not as rigorous as it once was but is open to development as culture changes. This happens as the Church enters into ecumenical dialogue and conversations with the world religions. In this process of identity clarification, Catholics reject religious relativism, reaffirm the unique role of Jesus in salvation, and share his message through evangelization.

Catechesis is central in establishing Catholic identity. Equally important is the need to celebrate the sacraments, especially Christ's eucharistic presence. Such core beliefs and practices ground Catholic identity. This establishes the basis for effective parish ministry, which is rooted in Jesus' teaching and the Christian vocation to proclaim God's kingdom.

## Addressing People's Needs

Pastoral ministry addresses people's needs. These are related to secondary, primary, and core meaning, which this section considers.

*Secondary meaning* is the meaning that functional things like clothes, a home, and money have in people's lives. We need them as we need adequate light, heat, and shelter. It is hard to function without an automobile, computer, or television set.

From a parish perspective, functional aspects of ministry include an efficiently organized catechetical program, well-prepared liturgies, adequate financial resources, a good lighting and sound system, sufficient parking, janitorial services, and a delivery system for various ministries. Without them it becomes difficult for a parish to address people's primary and core meaning.

*Primary meaning* is deeper than secondary meaning. We discover it in loving human relationships. For children, primary meaning is satisfied by parental love. Primary meaning is found in healthy relationships with parents, siblings, friends, spouses, and children. Hence, "community" in a parish setting is important. This is especially true when people are uprooted from family support systems through death, divorce, or job loss.

Culture is important in the quest for primary meaning. Ethnic roots connect us with a deep part of who we are in our pursuit of primary meaning. We experience such connections in ethnic celebrations and family pride. As America becomes more ethnically diverse, the need grows to recognize ethnic diversity in parishes. *Our Hearts Were Burning Within Us* says, "We live in a diverse multicultural society that offers us a rich experience of how the faith is lived, expressed, and celebrated in our own time" (p. 9).

Every person satisfies the need for primary meaning differently because the relational patterns of individuals, families, friends, and cultures differ. One person needs more affirmation than another. Sick people have greater need for support than the healthy. Some parents try to satisfy their children's need for parental affection through clothes or toys. These never satisfy their children's need for love and affection. Primary meaning cannot be realized through functional things. It must be addressed at the core level of human response. This level alone holds the key to fulfill need for primary meaning.

The search for *core meaning*, rooted in our spiritual quest, is innate to all human beings. It includes the need for love, trust, affection, roots, identity, and stability. The source from which this search springs moves us to ask questions like, "Why was I born?" "What is the meaning of my life?" "Why suffering?" "Why is there injustice in the world?" and "What will happen to me at death?" Such basic questions spring from the deepest dimension of our spiritual core where God dwells.

Religious traditions address such questions through their belief systems and ritual practices. Christians believe that Jesus lived and died for us to teach us how to live. He situates life's meaning not in money, possessions, and power (secondary meaning), but in love, forgiveness, and compassion (core meaning). He addressed core questions in light of God's plan for us. In Jesus' life we discover that the primary level of meaning, where we live our lives, requires a healthy balance of core and secondary life dimensions rooted in divine and human love. To address questions arising from the core level, religious traditions profess their fundamental beliefs in sacred stories, especially creation accounts, which recognize human limitation and the need for God.

Christianity teaches that Jesus answered our core questions. He lived out his mission and ministry on the level of primary relationships with Mary, Joseph, his friends, and his disciples. His life fulfilled the deepest aspirations of the core level, and his risen Spirit dwells at the core of who we are, inspiring us to turn away from sin and be faithful to the gospel.

Effective parishes address our basic needs for love, trust, and understanding by focusing on the core level. Functional approaches to ministry like well-organized programs, efficient office management, and comprehensive parish flow charts can only facilitate a parish's deeper efforts to satisfy people's core needs.

When primary needs are addressed at the core level, parish ministers help dispel parishioners' vulnerability by affording them trust, compassion, and hope. This was Jesus' way. He healed the broken, gave food to the hungry, and forgave sinners. His ministry centered on proclaiming God's kingdom, which touches the deepest core of human becoming. His Sermon on the Mount addressed people's needs and connected them with the kingdom of God.

## Recreating the Parish

The following aspects of ministry challenge parishes to reexamine their ministries in light of opportunities to recreate themselves in the spirit of Jesus, who came not to be served but to serve and to give his life for humankind.

### Creating Welcome: Communal, Social, and Familial Feelings about the Parish

People's hunger for roots creates a need for meaningful relationships. Responding to this need can be as simple as inviting a new neighbor in the apartment complex to come to a parish social or Mass. Effective parishes create such a welcoming atmosphere.

The success of some Protestant churches in attracting new members attests to the importance of a welcoming community. Within a week of her moving into a new apartment, Marci, a Catholic, had three invitations from Protestant churches to attend their services. One came from a flyer under her door, the second from information in her mailbox, and the third from a personal invitation of her apartment's manager. She never received a personal welcome from the neighboring Catholic Church even though she registered there. She did, however, begin receiving her weekly collection envelopes.

Identifying people who move into a neighborhood is not difficult. Their names are available from sales and rental listings, real estate transfer records, or the Internet.

## Vibrant Liturgies and Preaching

Catholic parishes can learn from the remarks of Frank, an enthusiastic vice president of a large corporation. He spoke of his megachurch of 25,000 registered members in the southwest United States, describing how his faith journey led him to it.

When asked why this Protestant church, which began ten years ago, is so successful, Frank replied, "I attribute our success to several factors. The congregation is subdivided into smaller groupings connected through a leadership team. We regard the church as a small spiritual city and govern it this way. It conducts sports leagues and other activities that are limited to church members. A community, even a family, spirit exists, which the large size does not change. In fact, our size provides the financial resources enabling us to reach out to the poor, visit the sick, and engage in missionary activity."

Frank said that a community atmosphere, in itself, is not enough. He continued, "The main thing that keeps us together is vibrant worship services, especially the preaching and music. The excellent preaching is conservative. The messages presented give direction and stability to our lives, which are often beset with change, pressure, uncertainty, immorality, and diversity. They connect us to the core of who we are. At the same time, the upscale music joins us with the fast-paced life that we experience everyday. This balance of music and preaching provides an interesting spiritual orientation in today's world." Frank then remarked, "Catholic churches could learn from our successes, for a high percentage of our members are former Catholics."

His words challenge parishes to acknowledge that community is not enough. People want to hear a message that relates to what they experience in their family, society, and workplace. They want to be challenged by the Word of God and celebrate it in ways that connect with their daily lives. The comments of this business executive contain valuable insights for Catholic parishes looking to blend different peoples into a vibrant faith community. He says that people search for a welcoming, community-minded parish, with vibrant liturgies, good catechesis, and excellent preaching.

## Solid Catechesis and Religious Formation

Today's parishes recognize the need for catechesis on all levels. *The Catechism of the Catholic Church* and the *General Directory for Catechesis* offer perspectives for parish catechesis. Because we live in a secular culture, religious formation is very important. Current social challenges, however, make it difficult to devise ways to help people appreciate their faith.

While *Parishes and Parish Ministries* reports a general decline in organized parish ministries from 1992 to 1997, a significant exception is found in religious education. In 1992, 85.0 percent of parishes offered organized religious education for children under fourteen. In 1997, the percentage rose to 96.8 percent. (pp. 16–17) This increase indicates an across-the-board recognition of the importance of quality religious education for everyone.

## A High Level of Care Especially at Key Life Moments

Rites of passage, like marriage and death, provide special opportunities to connect with people. Catholics who experience the Church's caring presence at traumatic moments, such as sickness and death, rarely leave the Church.

St. Bernard Parish made a commitment to bereavement ministry. Their ministers are people of faith, well prepared to handle the sensitive times surrounding sickness and death. After experiencing their compassion, family members often express their appreciation. One woman remarked, "The care I received after the death of my father solidified the weak commitment I had to the Catholic Church. Now I know the Church cares." On the other hand, some Catholics describe how lack of support at such times affected their faith. A Mormon woman, formerly a Catholic, said she left the church after a Catholic minister publicly rebuffed her brother in remarks made during his funeral. Such stories remind parish ministers to give special attention to family members of the sick and dying.

## Outreach to the Poor and Needy

The Old and New Testaments describe God's special concern for the needy. Brought to fruition in Jesus' ministry, this continues in the ministry of the Christian community. Parishes carry out Jesus' command to love sick and vulnerable people through their ministry to parishioners, missionary activities, and assistance to inner-city parishes. In addition to organized programs, parishes are called to minister to people's everyday needs.

Statistical data hints at a lessening of parish ministry to the poor. *Parishes and Parish Ministries* compares surveys from 1992 to 1997. The study reports that parish social services for individual needs dropped from 69.4 percent to 51.1 percent. Ministries intended to organize civic, neighborhood, and parish groups for social action and change dropped from 39.8 percent to 30.5 percent during the same period.

## *Accessibility to Parish Ministers, Especially the Pastor*

As parishes become more complex, many people get a recorded message or voice mail when they call the parish. Often such communications do not satisfy a parishioner's need to connect with another human being. To be more people friendly, St. Cecilia's Parish's secretary answers the phone during the day and transfers the calls to homes of volunteer parishioners in the evening. These volunteers often are senior citizens.

In some parishes it is hard to contact a parish minister even during the day. In discussing this issue one pastor remarked, "I agree that it is more preferable to have a live voice during office hours. Voice mail can be an effective tool to reach people when the office is closed. Our parish uses voice mail quite effectively. For example, in off-hours, the recorded message says that if it is an emergency and you need to have a priest paged, you punch 'one,' and the person is able to leave a message. Wherever I am, I can instantly respond to it, for that message sets off a pager. I have been at a parishioner's home having dinner on Sunday evening when my pager went off. When this happens, I call immediately and respond to whatever emergency there is. When I am driving from a meeting, for example, if people have left voice mail messages for me, I retrieve them and respond immediately rather than waiting until I return to the parish. If used properly, voice mail really does work and meets the needs of the parishioners."

If used at all times, however, answering services give the implication, "We are busy at this end of the telephone. We'll get back to you, when we have time. If you have an important issue, keep trying to get through to us." Often people hang up after being told on a recorder to press multiple extensions to get a parish minister. An excited parishioner with an emergency may not react well in such a situation. Parishes need to give the impression that they care about parishioners and to take seriously how people's phone calls are answered.

Many parishes would be more welcoming places if they dispensed with answering services during office hours. At other times, they can serve a useful purpose if no other option is feasible.

## Compassionate Leadership

Compassionate parish leaders make parishioners feel important. Their caring attitude invites people to approach them at troubled times. Such leaders focus on the core of who people are by giving them the impression, "No matter who you are or what you did, you are a child of God."

Addressing parishioner's core needs includes their need for connections, love, compassion, hope, trust, self-worth, and answers to their basic questions about life, suffering, death, and the afterlife. Parish leaders address such core needs by connecting parish ministry with Jesus' call to reach out to the poor, act justly, and share its resources with neighbors.

## Pastoral Suggestions

To effectively address parishioner's primary and core needs, the following suggestions are offered:

- Inquire of the diocese about the availability of a good instrument to survey parishioners' needs. If no such survey exists, ask a professional company or parish members to devise one for your parish.

- Once the above instrument is available, ask the parish council to canvass parishioners to ascertain their secondary, primary, and core needs. Include the needs of each age and ethnic group in the parish.

- Mail a survey to all parishioners asking them to return it in the Sunday collection basket. Inquire as to the best ways to answer parishioners' phone calls during and after office hours.

- Invite the liturgical committee to conduct an ongoing survey to ascertain the response of the parish to its liturgical music.

- Have the adult formation committee plan a lecture, discussion, or seminar centering on, "What does it mean to be Catholic today?" (The question of Catholic identity)

- Ask each specific ministry to address what are the most important rituals involved in the lives of those they serve.

- Ask the spiritual life committee to look into setting up a vocations committee to pray for vocations to the priesthood and religious life, to invite parishioners to suggest candidates to be contacted about considering these vocations, and to begin a monthly prayer session for vocations, including Benediction.

- Discuss at the parish council the wisdom of developing more small faith communities or support groups, such as Renew, prayer groups, and bible study sessions.

- Divide the parish into neighborhoods or blocks and appoint neighborhood captains to maintain viable communication with the larger parish.

- Form a parish activities committee to arrange for activities throughout the year aimed at specific groups in neighborhoods, including families and ethnic groups.
- Have the coordinator of the youth and young adult ministries study and recommend new ways to develop small-group support for teenagers and young adults.
- Appoint an ad hoc committee to investigate the need for small-group support for professional people like doctors, nurses, teachers, and businesspersons.
- Encourage parishioners to write the priest presider at Sunday Mass when his homily effectively connected the readings of the day with their lives.
- Encourage priests to include in their homilies on an ongoing basis the importance of adult faith formation.
- Ascertain from the social agencies or ecumenical groups serving your area what more the parish can do to help meet the needs of the poor.
- Have the parish social-action committee look into linking up with a poor inner-city parish or one in another country.
- Ask the parish staff to plan an afternoon of reflection for full-time and volunteer ministers at the beginning of Advent and Lent, centered on the tension spots in their personal lives and parish ministries, with the goal of reconciliation and forgiveness.

Meeting people's needs is at the heart of Jesus' ministry and parish ministry. This is discussed in Part Two of this book, which centers on evangelization the foundation of parish ministry. It begins with a clarification of Catholic evangelization in Chapter Four.

PART TWO

*Grounding the Vision—
Evangelization*

# 4.

# *Evangelization: The Heart of Parish Life and Ministry*

Little contact took place between the First Baptist Church and St. Jude's Roman Catholic Parish in a small rural town. In fact, strangers wondered if these congregations were Christian when they heard the hostile remarks made between members of each church at the local grocery store and beauty parlor.

No one remembers how the tension began. An old legend, going back over one hundred years, says that it began when one prominent member of each congregation argued over the ownership of a prize horse. At that time, respective church members began to squabble, which was accentuated over the years by growing differences about religious beliefs.

That was until a tornado hit town and completely destroyed the Baptist church. It also destroyed the homes and injured members of both congregations. Then a miracle happened. The townspeople began helping one another. For the first time in memory Catholics and Baptists worked together on common projects and no one paid attention to church affiliation. The Catholic congregation invited the Baptists to hold their services in St. Jude's Church and to use their parish facilities for meetings and bible study. Both communities joined in a concerted effort to rebuild the First Baptist Church. The climax occurred when Pastor Walker, the Baptist minister, Father Edgar, the Catholic priest, and their respective congregations joined for the rededication of the new Baptist church.

Sometimes it takes a tragedy to help Christians appreciate Jesus' command to forgive and to reach out to hurting people. What happened here is at the heart of Jesus' mission and the Church's ministry. When the Catholic and Baptist congregations joined in a spirit of love, they mutually shared Jesus' good news with one another.

Their sharing reflects the Church's belief about the parish's need to have unifying factors for its life and ministry. These may be as simple as joining together for a potluck dinner or as complex as joining together to handle a traumatic event like a tornado. For Christians, such events, rooted in Jesus' good news, is what evangelization is all about.

Parish organizational structure alone cannot be the unifier of a parish's vision and spirit. Like any organization, a parish sets up functional structures to unify its various ministries. The parish can have an efficiently organized flow chart and structures, but still not be effective in proclaiming God's Word.

A parish's mission transcends any flow chart. More is required to unify the complexities of parish life and connect various ministries into a unified whole. The "more" that is required centers around Jesus' message, as illustrated by what happened between the parishioners of St. Jude Parish and the First Baptist Church. Consequently, the answer to what is the unifier of parish life and ministry is found in the single word *evangelization,* a term many Catholics misunderstand.

Without the sharing of God's Word that evangelization proclaims, life seeps out of a parish. With it, new energy flows into the Christian community. We see evidence of this in the story of St. Jude's Parish described above. This chapter looks at The Meaning of Evangelization; Evangelization and the Kingdom; Evangelization and Ministry; Evangelization: the Responsibility of the Entire Christian Community; Evangelization: Family, Parish, and Work; and Pastoral Suggestions.

## The Meaning of Evangelization

Evangelization begins with hospitality. The welcoming community lays the groundwork for all evangelization. Without it, ministerial efforts languish. Evangelization embraces all the actions and words by which members of the Christian community announce the good news. In so doing, people's faith in Jesus can awaken, grow, and mature. Pope Paul VI indicates the wide scope of evangelization when he says, "For the Church, evangelizing means bringing the good news into all strata of humanity, and through its influence, transforming humanity from within and making it new...." (*Evangelii Nuntiandi* 18).

Consequently, "...*evangelization is a process fostering ongoing conversion within the Christian community that seeks to initiate people ever more deeply into the mystery of God's love (the kingdom), as it is manifested most fully in the dying and rising of Jesus*" (*Catholic Evangelization: The Heart of Ministry*, p. 7). As the *General Directory for Catechesis* says, "...Evangelization must be viewed as the process by which the church, moved by the spirit, proclaims and spreads the gospel throughout the entire world" (*GDC*, #48)

*Catholic Evangelization: the Heart of Ministry* says, "Evangelization is the invitation to accept the good news of

God's love. Evidence of God's love, which first comes from life itself and sets the stage for Jesus' revelation, can be referred to as *implicit evangelization*. Examples include, the beauty of creation, parental love, compassionate listening of a friend, or community life of a parish. Even if Jesus' name is not mentioned, evangelization happens in such implicit ways, thus preparing for more explicit manifestations of Jesus' saving word" (p. 7).

Implicit evangelization sets the stage for *explicit evangelization* that "...proclaims the role of Jesus, God, kingdom, and Church in God's plan of salvation and gives deeper insights into the God already present in implicit evangelization. This happens formally in a catechetical session, classroom, or study group; and informally when alone, with friends, or in the workplace" (p. 7). Consequently, explicit evangelization takes implicit evangelization one step further. For instance, Marta, a public hospital nurse, implicitly evangelizes through her compassionate care of a sick person. When the sick person asks her why she is so kind, and she reflects on her belief in Jesus and her call to be compassionate, as he was, Marta is explicitly evangelizing.

*Evangelization is not a separate ministry, but is central to all ministries. It is their heart, soul, and spirit, creating the climate for the ministries of Word, worship, and service.* In describing the process of evangelization, the *General Directory for Catechesis* says, "The process of evangelization, consequently, is structured in stages or 'essential moments': missionary activity directed toward nonbelievers and those who live in religious indifference; initial catechetical activity for those who choose the gospel and for those who need to complete or modify their initiation; pastoral activity directed toward the Christian faithful of mature faith in the bosom of the Christian community" (*GDC, #49*).

The above statement indicates that there is a *within* and *without* of evangelization as it pertains to the parish community. The *within* refers to those activities that initiate, assist, strengthen, and support the community itself. It includes ministries such as children's catechesis, bible study groups, and formal activities like worship and prayer. The *without* refers to activities in which the community reaches outside itself in missionary endeavors, ecumenical activities, and outreach to alienated Catholics, like the *Come Home Program*.

It is important to realize the broad scope of evangelization because people often assume that it is limited to the type that is called "missionary activity" (*GDC, #49*). Those regarding it in this way limit evangelization to inviting nonbelievers to follow Jesus or to join a church. This is one form of evangelization, but not its main focus. It also includes sharing Jesus' good news with nonpracticing Catholics, people with little knowledge of their faith, and committed Catholics desiring to deepen their conversion to the Lord.

Consequently, evangelization is the foundation of the lifelong process of conversion in which God's word is heard again and again. Every time a parent helps children appreciate God's Word by reading Bible stories or praying with them, the parent evangelizes. Every time a neighbor consoles another person with a kind gesture, the neighbor evangelizes. Every time a parish reaches out to the poor, the parish evangelizes. The Catholic approach to evangelization differs from the kind of evangelization that emphasizes hearing the Word of God and accepting Jesus Christ once and for all in a definitive moment of being converted or saved.

## Evangelization and the Kingdom

Jesus proclaimed the good news of the kingdom. His mission announced the kingdom and his ministry brought it to fulfillment. His concern for all people, especially the poor, sinners, and alienated, responded to that mission, which climaxed in his dying, rising, and sending of the Spirit. This kingdom exists today in mystery. It is a kingdom where the first are last, and the last, first. The sign of its presence is forgiveness and service to the poor.

Reflecting on God's forgiveness reminds us that God commands us to forgive those who hurt us. This is difficult and makes little earthly sense. Why should we forgive those who offend us? We should forgive them because we are Christians and continue Jesus' evangelizing ministry.

Jim's story exemplifies the need to forgive. He likes to collect antiques. One time, a person took his best old bottle. He fretted and wondered what to do. At the time, he did nothing, but he never forgot about it. Years later, Jim realized how forgiving the person who took his bottle made sense only in light of God's forgiveness of him.

Who knows why the person stole the bottle? Christians forgive because they have been forgiven. The willingness to forgive is a strong testimony of our faith in the kingdom to come, where God judges the deeds of every person.

Forgiveness is a sign of God's kingdom. It is at the heart of evangelization. Proclaiming God's kingdom of forgiveness is every Christian's responsibility. *Our Hearts Were Burning Within Us* says, "Every disciple of the Lord Jesus shares in this mission" (p. 1). Since the Christian community continues Jesus' work, the Church's mission and ministry focuses on the kingdom. Reflecting on the parish's mission in light of Jesus' call to forgive, we see how petty jealousy and failure to reconcile can split a parish community. A parish gives little witness to evangelization when its members, especially the leaders, refuse to forgive.

St. Margaret's Parish witnessed the consequences of negative bickering on its pastoral council. It got so bad that an outside priest, Father Bert, was asked to moderate a meeting of this group at a retreat house on a Sunday afternoon. The negativity showed itself immediately after the meeting began, when the group started to argue. Right away, Father Bert said, "I did not come to hear this sort of thing. It's a beautiful day outside, and I'd prefer to be there or to watch a football game on television. It's no use going on as we are. You have a choice. Go home and enjoy the day or take several hours and walk around this retreat setting and think of what has been happening. Ask yourself what Jesus taught you about forgiveness and how it applies in this situation. I'll leave the choice up to you. What do you want to do?" Too embarrassed to leave, the group decided to stay. Then someone said, "It's Sunday afternoon, and we have not attended Mass. We were scheduled to celebrate it here at 5:30 with you and this group. Are we still going to do so?" Father Bert replied, "Frankly, I don't know. I have difficulty celebrating the Eucharist—the great act of forgiveness—with a group that has so much animosity among themselves. We won't decide now, but when we come back at 5:00, we'll discuss whether we are worthy to celebrate the Eucharist." When the group returned, the tone was different, and they decided that they wanted to work on reconciliation. The pastoral council celebrated the Eucharist that evening and met into the night with a new sense of purpose and a different spirit. For the first time they listened to one another. New life begins when people are willing to forgive.

The Church is not the kingdom, yet the Christian community is intimately related to it. In the preceding episode the pastoral council was part of the Christian community but was not living according to the dictates of the kingdom. It was the kingdom message of forgiveness that called this group back to the spirit of the Gospels. Vatican II recalls the bonds that link Jesus, Church, and kingdom. It says, "The mystery of the holy Church is manifest in its very foundation. The Lord Jesus Christ set it on its course by preaching the Good News, that is, the coming of the Kingdom of God, which, for centuries, had been promised in the Scriptures: 'The time is fulfilled, the kingdom of God is at hand.'" *(Lumen Gentium 5)*. Consequently, all parish evangelization is measured against Jesus' teaching on the kingdom.

To ensure fidelity to Jesus' command, he sends the Spirit. We gauge whether parish activities are of the Spirit by measuring them in light of the scriptures and the Church's living tradition. The parish fails to reflect Jesus' good news if its life and ministry do not mirror the kingdom. *Sharing the Light of Faith* relates the Church's mission to the kingdom when it says, "The Church continues the mission of Jesus: prophet, priest, and servant king. Its mission, like his, is essentially one—to bring about God's kingdom—but this one mission has three aspects: proclaiming and teaching God's word, celebrating the sacred mysteries, and serving the people of the world" (#30). Then it goes on to say that three aspects of the Church's mission correspond to and exist to serve it. These "are three ministries: the ministry of the word, the ministry of worship, and the ministry of service. In saying this, however, it is important to bear in mind that the several elements of the Church's mission are inseparably linked in reality (each includes and implies the others), even though it is possible to study and discuss them separately" (#30).

The preceding statements describe the ministry of Jesus and the Church in terms of the ministries of Word, worship, and service. When a parent teaches a child about God, the parent is a minister of the *Word*. When a catechist distributes the communion cup at his or her class's first communion Mass, that person is a minister of *worship*. When a parishioner works at the parish's soup kitchen, he or she is a minister of *service*. The ministry of service is a special prerogative of the laity, especially in their Christian witness in the world.

Word, worship and service are aspects of evangelization. These ministries do not operate in isolation from each other. Neither do we classify catechesis, liturgy, or service projects exclusively in the categories of Word, worship, and service. Such ministries interpenetrate each other. They clarify God's revelation and continued communication through the evangelizing mission of the Church.

At St. Anthony's Parish, catechists, liturgists, and service ministers work with the pastor and support staff as friends and co-ministers. Their concern for one another and commitment to evangelization blend the various ministries into a unified testimony of Christ's ministry. This parish's attitude is a far cry from the dissensions experienced among some parish staffs as they compete for position and resources. One parish minister asked, "Why is there often a lack of charity among the people who worked on the staffs in parishes where I have served?"

All parish ministries relate to a parish's mission. In reflecting on catechetical, liturgical, and service ministries, *Sharing the Light of Faith* says, "It [catechetical ministry] is a form of the ministry of the word, which proclaims and teaches. It leads to and flows from the ministry of worship, which sanctifies through prayer and sacrament. It supports the ministry of service...." (#32).

A parish reflects God's kingdom and its own commitment to evangelization in setting priorities, developing parish ministries, and maintaining good staff relations. A sign of how a parish incorporates evangelization's kingdom message into its life and ministry is the degree to which it provides ministerial opportunities for persons with disabilities. A person with disabilities remarked that her parish refused to allow anyone who used a wheelchair to read at Mass or distribute holy communion. This hurt her deeply for she felt called by God to offer her ministerial gifts as a reader or communion distributor. The parish was not willing to accommodate her by putting a handicapped ramp into the sanctuary or by making other provisions to enable her to minister. It was possible to do so in this church, but the parish leaders did not want to bother.

In contrast to this parish, St. Mel's Parish does a remarkable job in assisting both parishioners and ministers with disabilities. Movable ramps allow such ministers to move freely from the body of the church to the altar, ambo, and minister's chairs. An electric device on the ambo moves it up and down at a flip of a switch to accommodate readers who use wheelchairs. Special provisions exist for the hearing- and sight-impaired.

When a parish does not welcome the hearing-impaired by providing a minister who assists them at Mass, or catechesis for the developmentally delayed, or ramps or elevators for those in wheelchairs, these people often go elsewhere where they feel welcome. They may join Protestant churches, avail themselves of ministry in another Catholic parish, or not go to church at all. Each parish is responsible for the spiritual needs of persons with special needs. Like everyone else, they want to feel part of the liturgy. This begins with welcome, as the parish looks for various ways to make them blend into the community as important, participants.

Today's parish continues the 2000-year-old tradition of Christian communities in giving testimony to the power of Jesus' evangelizing mission. Like him, the parish proclaims God's good news to its members and beyond to the world. As the *General Directory for Catechesis* says, "Indeed the primordial mission of the Church is to proclaim God and to be his witness before the world" (*GDC*, #23). To be faithful to its mission, the parish must reflect Jesus in its words and actions. There is only one Christian mission—that of Jesus Christ. A parish's mission images Jesus' mission of proclaiming the good news.

Every Christian is responsible to carry out Jesus' mission. As *The Vocation and the Mission of the Lay Faithful in the Church and in the World* says, "The Church's mission of salvation in the world is realized not only by the ministers in virtue of the Sacrament of Orders but also by all the lay faithful; indeed, because of their Baptismal state and their specific vocation, in the measure proper to each person, the lay faithful participate in the priestly, prophetic, and kingly mission of Christ" (#23).

## Evangelization and Ministry

Evangelization, the driving force of discipleship and Church ministry, is centered on proclaiming the good news of Jesus' living, dying, rising, and sending of the Spirit. The paschal mystery is the focus of this ministry as the risen Lord continues to bring about God's kingdom through the believing Church. Evangelization is a lifelong process, and conversion is being changed by the good news that evangelization proclaims. The following story illustrates how people are changed by the good news of God's love.

Ellen served as a lay chaplain in a large, mid-West Catholic hospital. She had been under unusual pressure due to a staff shortage. Deciding she needed time to recuperate, she signed up for a retreat. When she arrived, she was met by Jim, a man who identified himself as a part-time gardener. During her stay there, she found few other staff people who made her feel welcome. One day another retreatant told a tale of hurt and abandon. The group moderator did not know how to respond to her, so he just left the room. Jim spoke briefly to her.

The next day, the troubled woman repeated her story and again the moderator didn't respond. At that point, Jim said, "Maybe I can help if I tell my story. For years, I was a drunk who hurt my wife, children, and myself through my drinking. It was always the same. I'd drink, leave home, and come back a few days later and beg my wife to take me back. Finally she said that if it happened again, I would be on my own until I really changed. The next time I returned, my suitcase was on the porch.

"I moved to another city and wandered the streets for almost a year. During this time, I never lost faith in God, often finding myself sitting alone in a Catholic church. But the drinking continued. One day, I sat in a tavern on the barstool. A girl danced near the bar, a few feet away. She asked me for money. At that point, I became disgusted with myself and happened to look down at my pitcher of beer before me. In it, I clearly saw an image of the crucifix. Whether it was shadows from the room or a real miracle, I'll never know. Either way, it was a miracle. I thought of what Jesus did for me, and a surge of courage came into my heart.

I left that half-filled pitcher of beer on the bar and took a bus home.

"Soon, I was standing in front of my door begging my wife and kids to take me back. I told them the story and they welcomed me back home. Immediately I got a job and two years later, when my children had left the house for college, I asked my wife if we could work to establish a place for troubled youth. It has happened, and now I manage this home." Monica, his wife, standing nearby, affirmed all he said. She commented, "Jim has never taken another drink. We have very little money, and we spend most of our money on the troubled youth. Often, when we are down to our last dollar, someone gives us money. Jim says that if we have faith in God and one another, God takes care of the rest." Jim's story helped the troubled woman. She, too, began to refocus her life around faith in the Lord Jesus Christ.

Jim's story reminds us that brokenness occurs in every person's life. So does the promise of resurrection for those who have faith. This unfolding drama of the paschal mystery, embedded in flesh and blood, is the heart of evangelization. It gives pastoral ministries a reason and purpose. Christians evangelize by continuing the saving actions of Christ.

In proclaiming the dying and rising of Jesus, evangelization energizes Christian endeavors, reminding us of our mission to live out God's kingdom in our homes, neighborhood, and workplace. All ministry is rooted in the lifeblood of evangelization; without it, individual or institutional efforts to proclaim the word, celebrate it, or serve others lack the dynamism promised by the good news. As John Paul II says in the *Gospel of Life*, "Evangelization is an all-embracing, progressive activity through which the Church participates in the prophetic, priestly and royal mission of the Lord Jesus

Christ. It is therefore inextricably linked to *preaching, celebration and the service of charity.* Evangelization is a *profoundly ecclesial act,* which calls all the various workers of
the Gospel to action, according to their individual charisms
and ministry" (§78).

Evangelization, therefore, is the proclamation of the
lived reality of Jesus' dying, rising, and sending of the Spirit.
It is the marrow of all Christian ministry providing the
dynamism for the ministries of Word, worship and service.
These ministries are inseparably linked. They never exist in
isolation but constantly interpenetrate one another, even
though in various Church ministries, or at a given time or
place, one or the other may be given higher priority. Their
effectiveness depends upon whether or not they are
enlivened by the lived reality of an evangelized and evangelizing community.

## Evangelization: The Responsibility
## of the Entire Christian Community

Although evangelization pertains to the entire Christian
life, its lived reality in a community of Word, worship, and
service constitutes the heart of the Church's witness to the
presence of Jesus' ongoing dying and rising in the Christian
community. All parish organizations, structures, and programs exist to help the Christian community evangelize
through the ministry of the entire Church. Hence, evangelization is a part of a parish's sporting events and financial
committee just as it is the heart of the parish's catechetical
and liturgical life.

Parishes need to develop an evangelizing vision that is
rooted in the kingdom and based on the parish's uniqueness.
Such a vision is family centered and holistic, integrating

every parish ministry, blending them into an authentic response to individual and community needs. This is not the responsibility of a few professionals alone. Rather, every Christian by virtue of baptism is entrusted with the awesome task of sharing Jesus' good news of salvation. The spirit of the entire community has far more impact on parish evangelization than the efforts of the pastor or a few parish ministers working alone. To generate such parish response, the pastor plays a vital role as the symbol that evangelization is happening in the entire parish community.

Viewing the parish as a community of smaller communities that gather to hear God's word, celebrate it in the liturgy, and support one another helps us see the flexibility needed to evangelize groups within the parish. To facilitate ministerial effectiveness, each parish needs a well-articulated vision of evangelization to ensure ministry to all parishioners and to those beyond the parish. Pope John Paul II reflects on the wide scope of evangelization in the words, "Evangelization is not only the Church's living teaching, the first proclamation of the faith *(kērygma)* and instruction, formation of the faith (catechesis); it is also the entire *wide-ranging commitment to reflect on revealed truth,* a commitment expressed from the very beginning in the *works of the Fathers* in the East and in the West" (*Crossing the Threshold of Hope,* p. 107).

## Evangelization: Family, Parish, and Work

Evangelization, seen from a dialogical perspective, happens in three chief settings, namely, family, parish, and work. Here, evangelization manifests itself in the ordinary experiences of our lives. We learn how to evangelize in these contexts especially by being sensitive to those whom Jesus refers to as "the little ones."

This happened as Mary observed an elderly woman struggle up Elm Avenue. She veered from side to side as she tapped her cane. Immediately, Mary realized that the woman was a resident of the Christian home for the blind further up the street.

Soon Mary saw a big young man with a huge smile approach the woman. He put his strong arm around her shoulders. The blind woman recognized the gesture, for she did not recoil but smiled in grateful thanks. As Mary watched them, she noticed that the woman and the man, both now smiling profusely, walked up the street supporting each other. She realized that both of them were blind and she thought, "The blind leading the blind." Theirs was physical blindness, but beneath it was the spiritual wisdom that Paul referred to when he said that eyes have not seen, nor ears heard, what God has prepared for the people who love him (1 Cor 2:9).

The blind man's gesture in helping the old woman is what evangelization invites all Christians to imitate. Evangelization recognizes human brokenness and asks Christians to respond to it in the spirit of love.

The evangelization process happens in the interplay of world, family, and church. Each contributes to the manifestation of the good news. This implies that God's kingdom comes through family, friends, marketplace, culture, school, and work. Parish evangelists are found in every walk of life. They evangelize in their homes, neighborhood, or marketplace. As evangelizers, they share the Word of God with others. The Christian evangelizes by illuminating God's presence, already at work in people's hearts and manifested through scripture, Church teaching, and the lives of faithful Christians.

The family, world, and Church are subjects, not objects, of evangelization. They mutually enrich one another. When this dialogue happens, the good news remains alive and dynamic. The parish offers to this dialogue a vision of the kingdom as revealed by Jesus and taught by Christian tradition. This vision leads to acts of service and celebration with the family and the world. The parish acknowledges itself as a partner in the evangelization process, especially as the parish relates to the family.

"Family" includes traditional, single-parent, blended, and divorced families as well as other configurations. It is important to recognize these various groupings and to avoid advertising, programming, lectures, workshops, and preaching that presuppose only a nuclear structure. Many parishes do creative things in their bulletin announcements and posters to include all kinds of family configurations.

Increasingly, the influx of ethnic groups into a parish raises another challenging issue—that of multilingual parishes. Parishes may be challenged to provide parallel bulletins, activities, programs, and catechetical opportunities in two or more languages. The language issue transcends age, economic condition, culture, race, and marital status. In fact, multicultural challenges can exist within a language group: Filipinos, African Americans, Irish, Poles, and Italians may all speak English, but their cultures and customs are quite different. Similarly, Spaniards, Cubans, Puerto Ricans, Chileans, Mexicans, and Salvadorans may all speak Spanish, but their cultures and customs are quite different. While no specific answers exist to meet such challenges, sensitive pastoral leaders need to be conscious of them and devise ways to address them.

The parish and individual families need to have healthy communication with each other. If this does not happen, little communication may result. From the parish perspective, certain elements recommend themselves to ensure reciprocity with family and world, necessary for effective evangelization.

Evangelization begins when families of various kinds feel at home in the parish. This applies to regular parish members and visitors alike. It is especially important during transition periods, such as birth, death, marriage, divorce, adolescence, and young adulthood. Many people going through a divorce feel parish support; others feel shunned. Youth frequently comment that they do not feel welcome in their parish, saying that what happens there is for adults and children, not for them.

Effective parishes recognize the centrality of the family. Consequently, family-oriented parishes address many everyday spiritual needs, including religious education, home catechesis, prayers, and devotions—as well as provide help coping with the demands of society and work. It also means that parishes limit the responsibilities family members are asked to assume in parish ministry.

When parishes see the family as the subject rather than the object of evangelization, ministerial efforts shift. Real commitment is given to families, including singles, rather than to the institution itself. Affirming single people and providing support systems gives them renewed confidence in the parish. Since every parish includes many unmarried people, efforts must be made to make them feel welcome in the wider community.

It is obvious the parish is a network of diverse communities and individuals, not a homogenous mass of people. Children, youth, young adults, parents, singles, divorced people, senior citizens, ethnically and economically diverse parishioners, clubs, organizations, neighborhoods, and prayer groups are some of the natural groupings in every parish. *Our Hearts Were Burning Within Us* emphasizes particular sensitivity to various cultures within a parish. It says, "Work directly with people of each racial or ethnic group to find ways to affirm or renew values expressed in their family traditions, social customs, and popular devotions. Special attention must be paid to those groups that are most easily forgotten: particularly those who are elderly, those who are living with handicapping conditions, those who are alienated from society" (p. 28).

With today's growing ethnic diversity, this comment invites ministers to utilize the various customs and traditions to enrich the parish. For example, at Pentecost, Advent, and Christmas, different customs from various ethnic traditions can enrich the liturgy itself and the devotional life surrounding it. Many liturgists incorporate ethnic languages or customs. This affirms the ethnic peoples within the parish and teaches the wider community new and beautiful ways to celebrate the main feasts. Such diversity is strengthening. But to tap into the gifts inherent in different age and ethnic groups requires an open style of leadership and clear direction. Without direction, diversity becomes confusion. With it, diversity brings creativity and new life. Catholics are invited to recognize the spirit of the risen Lord ministering through the gifts of the various members of the Body of Christ. For this to happen, parishes can develop a mutuality of ministries based on the diverse gifts of their parishioners.

Evangelization, strengthened by a mutuality of ministries, is effective when parishioners see their call as rooted in the Christian community. They become aware of their call to be disciples of Jesus in the ordinary experiences of life and to grow in this awareness by reaching out to others in times of sickness, divorce, job loss, or death. Such ministry is celebrated in all the sacraments, especially in the rites of Christian initiation.

To maximize parish evangelization, church leaders need to work together for a common purpose centered on the kingdom of God. In this endeavor, catechesis is complemented by liturgy, with ministerial service as the outgrowth of listening to and celebrating God's Word. For this to happen, a parish constantly prioritizes and redirects efforts toward ministry to all its members.

## Pastoral Suggestions

Specific issues arise from the considerations of this chapter. They include the following:

- Suggest to the pastor that he encourage parishioners at a Sunday Mass before Advent and Lent to invite a lapsed family member or friend back to church.
- Invite the members of the parish youth group to ask one of their friends to attend a special youth activity, such as a project to help the needy, a cookout, or a picnic.
- Have the parish staff arrange an afternoon or evening of recollection for parish-council and finance-council members, centering on their role in creating an evangelizing parish.
- Ask the senior citizen group to arrange a day of prayer for the elderly, centering on sharing the good news with sick parish members.
- Recommend to the parish council that an evaluation be done of the way secretaries, custodians, and ushers reflect the parish's spirit of evangelization.

- Encourage all religion teachers of children to emphasize the parish's role in evangelizing others through missionary outreach by having the children collect money for a particular mission and send a letter with it, indicating their prayers and support.

- Ask the pastoral council to arrange to put a small container at the ends of every church pew containing a welcome card for visitors to sign.

- Examine the best way to minister to the hearing-impaired at liturgical functions. This may be to sign from the altar or to have another person next to them sign at the Mass.

- Put a suggestion in the parish bulletin or Web page giving specific tips to parents on how to evangelize in their families.

- Ask the parish education commission to invite a speaker to address the parish during Lent on the new Catholic evangelization.

The perspectives on evangelization described in this chapter are closely related to the fundamental pillars of parish life. These are discussed in the next chapter, "Evangelization and the Four Pillars of Parish Life."

# 5.

# *Evangelization and the Four Pillars of Parish Life*

The fish fry on the Fridays of Lent plays a central role at St. Augustine's Parish. It is more than an opportunity to make a few dollars for the parish's outreach to the poor in the neighborhood. Those preparing and serving the meals have become a community of fun and support, and their friendship goes beyond the Fridays of Lent. Those attending the event fill the cafeteria with conversation. They include parishioners, neighbors, visitors, and people of various religious denominations. Many teenagers assemble in the back of the hall to discuss the week's happenings. While the people eat, the pastor and parish ministers move around the tables, learning what is going on in the lives of those who come. Many future appointments to discuss parishioners' problems begin this way.

No formal evangelization happens at the fish fry, but the entire event illustrates the powerful witness of informal evangelization. The Lord's good news is incorporated in the hospitality and enthusiasm of those who work at the event. This time together is a unifying factor of the parish's life during Lent.

Evangelization permeates every segment of parish life, but its dynamism is focused in four essential dimensions, which we refer to as the four pillars of parish life. They are a parish's *mission, members, ministry,* and *management.* When these dimensions mutually interact in the spirit of Christ's gospel, the parish becomes a loving community. The parish is not a pillar in itself, but it results from loving relationships created through the mutual connections among the four pillars. No parish can set out with a plan to create community. Community happens when Jesus' message is effectively proclaimed, acted out, and managed.

Every parish exists to carry out its *mission,* which mirrors Jesus' mission. This it does through its *ministry,* accomplished by its parish *members.* They extend the parish's mission and ministry to the broader society. To ensure a well-ordered community, *management* serves the parish's mission, ministry, and members. This chapter considers these four pillars and then offers Pastoral Suggestions.

## The Four Pillars: Mission, Members, Ministry, and Management

Mission, members, ministry, and management constitute the four pillars of parish life. Although they are connected, each one is treated separately.

### *Mission*

The first pillar of parish life is its *mission,* which a parish's mission statement reflects. The parish's mission takes its origin from Jesus' mission, which Luke articulates during Jesus' visit to the Nazareth synagogue at the beginning his public ministry. In the synagogue, Jesus unrolled the scroll of Isaiah and read:

> "The Spirit of the Lord is upon me,
>     because he has anointed me

> to bring good news to the poor.
> He has sent me to proclaim release to the captives
> and recovery of sight to the blind,
>> to let the oppressed go free,
>> to proclaim the year of the Lord's favor."
>> (Luke 4:18–19)

When finished, Jesus indicated that these words were fulfilled in him. Outraged at this comment, synagogue members challenged him, cast him from the building, and tried to kill him. Jesus' actions in the synagogue proclaimed God's kingdom, which was announced at his Annunciation, witnessed in his birth, lived out during his life, and brought to fruition through his death on the cross.

The kingdom proclaimed by Jesus is the focus of all evangelization. It brings life, freedom, healing, and hope. This was announced by the prophets, fulfilled in Jesus, and continued through the Christian community. Jesus' mission reveals God's love, manifested in his special concern for poor, humble people. It reminds us that effective evangelization cannot happen if we neglect them.

Parish evangelization communicates love flowing from the love that inspired God to create the universe and redeem humankind. It urges parishioners to develop an attitude of evangelization when they prepare a liturgy, work at a fish fry, or coach an athletic team. Such an attitude is centered primarily in ministering to families and society. Evangelizing parishioners are sensitive to opportunities to support co-workers, encourage neighbors, and help their loved ones come closer to God.

Buoyed up by such an attitude, the parish becomes a beacon of faith, source of hope, and home for confused, disillusioned, and hurting individuals. It offers God's love to young, old, weak, strong, black, brown, white, yellow, and red people. It invites them to celebrate God's love and discover life's meaning by knowing Jesus and joining the parish.

Humans need love, indicated by a remark from Lisa, a pastoral minister, when she reported the findings of a series of family visitations. She said, "Our parish recently completed home visitations for families whose children had been baptized or had received first Eucharist or celebrated confirmation during the past year. In scheduling these visits, it was hard for families to take the time to meet with us."

She described how parish visitors met healthy and hurting families from various ethnic and socioeconomic backgrounds. Most of them were faith-filled, loving families working successfully to balance modern-day pressures.

Lisa continued, "We encountered families who struggled to survive. We heard stories of working parents, divorce, drugs, financial stress, pain, rejection, and fear. People discussed how society's fast pace, materialism, and pressures affected them, mentioning that they had little time for enjoyment, family life, and God."

These visitations led Lisa to conclude that parish evangelization efforts had to concentrate on developing parish attitudes that center on family and work needs. The visitations also highlighted the influence of secular society on these families and challenged the parish to come up with effective ways to share Jesus' good news, as happens in the "Elizabeth" ministry that reaches out to new mothers.

Sorting out the ramifications of developing a new focus for evangelization is difficult. It takes prayer, fasting, and wisdom. Openness to the Spirit helps parishes ascertain the meaning, depths, and implications of their call to evangelize in light of the gospel. These efforts begin with an awareness of the parish's responsibility to proclaim God's kingdom. Without it, parish ministry remains incomplete and shallow.

## Members

The second pillar of the parish is the *members* of the parish community. Jesus called twelve apostles as leaders of his disciples. After his resurrection, the followers of Jesus lived out his mission in community. The parish community continues his mission through its evangelizing ministry that communicates Jesus' kingdom message through the gifts of its members. These include the "order of the faithful" who are fully initiated into the Church through the sacraments of baptism, confirmation, and Eucharist, and the "order of the catechumens" who have been received into the Church but have not been fully initiated.

Although parish evangelization focuses on parish members, it cannot be presumed that all of them are committed, active Catholics. Many are seekers who are searching for their identity. They look for a message and community that will feed them spiritually.

Parishes must be open to all people who desire to hear Jesus' good news. This is illustrated in Sara's story. She was a short, olive-skinned woman who came to a parish meeting. Her clothing, hairstyle, and mode of speaking were different. She stumbled over words and spoke in incomplete sentences. Initially, those present wondered if she had a learning disability.

Soon it became apparent to those in attendance that Sara had limited knowledge of the English language. After the meeting the pastoral associate learned that she had fled persecution in a Near Eastern country after civil officials discovered that she belonged to a small religious assembly frowned upon by the government. Eventually she came to the United States. Sara obtained a doctorate in a scientific field but was unable to find employment because difficulties between her native country and the United States prohibited her from getting job clearance.

Sara became Catholic while working on her degree at a large California state university. When asked if she had gone through the Rite of Christian Initiation of Adults process, she replied sadly, "No. I never felt supported by the Catholic community. Many Catholics, even church ministers, looked down on me because I appeared to be different."

When asked what influenced her to become Catholic, she said, "While in graduate school an old priest, sensing my difficulties, was good to me. After I got to know him, I asked him why he was so kind to me. He told me about Jesus, and how he patterned his life on him. Together, we studied the Bible, especially Jesus' teachings. Eventually, he baptized me and brought me into the Church." The priest affirmed Sara's beautiful gifts, unrecognized by many Catholics who never looked beyond her appearances or into her heart.

From Sara's story we learn that Jesus' message is never shared in a vacuum. If she had not met the priest, Sara would not have accepted Jesus as her Lord. The priest influenced her, not because he was a priest, but because he was a Christian. His response to Sara is the responsibility of every Christian. His example shows how the power of Jesus' love prevailed in her life.

The second pillar, the members, reminds us that parishes are made up of "people." Solid parish evangelization assumes that parishioners are the heart of its ministry and the ground where Jesus' mission grows. Parish evangelization invites the poor and broken as well as the rich and strong to find life's deepest meaning in Christ.

Jesus' message spreads when parishioners evangelize. A corporate leader evangelizes when she is honest and just in her dealings with employees. A financial officer evangelizes when he refuses to alter the books to cover up a shortfall. Catholic neighbors evangelize when they invite a Chinese couple that just moved into the area to their home for a welcoming evening. In the course of one such visit Mark, the host, asked the Chinese couple to come with him and his family to their parish for a social. A month after this event, they attended Mass. Next, the new neighbors entered the RCIA. Today, they are active Catholics. This is Catholic evangelization in action. It began with a simple welcome to the neighborhood. Parish leaders need to help parishioners see how evangelization can be part of everyday life.

Evangelization needs to motivate every parish activity, including liturgy, religious education, budget decisions, council agendas, ministry and social-outreach functions. When this happens, the parish lives the social-justice message that it preaches. If parishioners live out Jesus' kingdom message in their homes, with friends, and at work, the parish becomes an evangelizing community.

## Ministry

*Ministry,* the third pillar of the parish, links evangelization directly with Jesus' ministry. He fulfilled his mission through his ministry, which included his deeds, words, and the way he lived his life. His evangelizing ministry climaxed with his passion, death, and resurrection. Throughout Jesus' life he identified with peoples' needs, treated them as God's children, and gave them hope. The parish's ministry is the way it lives out its mission as reflected in its mission statement. The overall impression a parish conveys sets the tone for its ministerial actions. If this tone is welcoming and positive, people are more inclined to connect with the parish. Ministry begins with welcome, which was absent in the story that Sara told about her experience with the Catholic community. It was present, however, in the old priest's hospitality. If the broader parish fails, most people are not as fortunate as Sara in finding someone to show them Jesus' message.

Parish ministry centers on Word, worship, and service, which interlock to embrace the totality of effective ministry. They further God's kingdom through proclaiming God's word, celebrating the sacred mysteries, and serving the people.

## Ministry of the Word

The ministry of the Word proclaims Jesus as Lord; its key aspects are catechesis and preaching. Both are about conversion, namely, bringing people to a deeper realization of God's love and its implications for practical living.

Catechesis includes more than imparting basic teachings of the Catholic faith. While focusing on the basic teachings of the faith, its long-range significance depends on the degree that a person internalizes such teachings by appreciating its relationship with life and liturgy. This internalization process is central to catechesis.

Seen in this light, catechesis is a "process that invites a person to hear, understand, interiorize, and respond to God's word in acts of service and celebration" (*Parish Catechetical Ministry*, p. 3). Pope John Paul II says that catechesis includes efforts "to make disciples, to help people to believe that Jesus is the son of God, so that believing they might have life in his name, and to educate and instruct them in this life and thus build up the body of Christ" (*Catechesis in Our Time*,

1). Catechesis bears fruit when it strengthens personal faith and incorporates people into a faith community. Based in the family, catechesis is supported through parish ministry.

Informal catechesis includes activities that reflect God's Word in some way. A mother's teaching her child about Jesus, an employees' testimony about the value of daily scripture reading, God-centered service projects, family prayer, and liturgy all have catechetical aspects. Such activities set the tone for systematic catechesis.

Systematic catechesis includes activities that are deliberate, intentional, and structured. It teaches God's Word and helps people commit to its message. While catechesis involves more than teaching basic facts of the faith, knowledge of these basics is important. The publication of the *Catechism of the Catholic Church* challenges parishes to focus on preparing catechists and ensuring that systematic catechesis includes clear teaching about Jesus' and the Church's message.

*Our Hearts Were Burning Within Us* emphasizes the priority of adult catechesis or faith formation when it says, "We are convinced that the energy and resources we devote to adult faith formation will strengthen and invigorate all the charisms that adults receive and the activities they undertake, in the Church and in society, to serve the Gospel of Christ and the people of today" (p. 13). In reflecting on how to accomplish this goal, the bishops go on to say, "Whatever model is used, adult faith formation should always actively challenge participants to get involved with their own faith journey—passive listening is never enough; the goal is always conversion" (p. 26).

Knowledge of basic Church teaching is an aspect of faith formation on all levels. It helps illuminate people's experience in their journey of conversion. The *Catechism of the*

*Catholic Church* provides a summary of Church teachings to assist pastors, catechetical leaders, principals, and catechists. In using the catechism, catechists need to adapt its content by employing language and methods suitable to those being catechized. This is a special responsibility of national catechisms, religion textbooks, and catechists (*CCC*, §24).

Many parish activities teach God's Word in planned or organized ways. These include Catholic school, sacramental preparation programs, parish school of religion sessions, youth catechesis, formal instruction in the RCIA, planned scripture study, and adult catechetical opportunities. Systematic catechesis can occur in a church, parish hall, classroom, home, or community center. Regardless of the setting, its regular and systematic nature relates God's Word to peoples' experiences, thus enabling them to interiorize its message and respond in acts of service and celebration.

Preaching, likewise, is a ministry of the Word. The only time most Catholics hear God's Word proclaimed is during Sunday liturgy. The presider is to convey it in a meaningful way so that the faithful may apply its wisdom to their lives. Preaching the gospel is central to priestly ministry. When conveying its message effectively, a priest continues the ministry of Jesus and the early disciples.

## Ministry of Worship

The ministry of worship is an important dimension of the evangelization process. It centers on the paschal mystery and celebrates Jesus' ongoing dying and rising. Like catechesis, the ministry of worship has informal and formal or systematic aspects. Informally, families praise God through mutual love, home prayers, and liturgical practices. When parishioners gather for Mass or other liturgical rituals, they formally join the broader Christian community in celebrating the God they honor in their homes and daily lives.

Christian liturgy is "the communal celebration of the ongoing dying and rising of Jesus by people who are called together by the spirit to remember the continued gift of God's love, to engage in rituals that commemorate the Paschal mystery, and to respond in service to the permanent reality of God's spirit" (*Parish Catechetical Ministry,* p. 4). While there are many prayerful liturgical celebrations, some Catholics indicate that Sunday eucharistic celebrations do not meet their needs. This may happen for a variety of reasons, including poor liturgical preparation, insipid homilies, or failure to appreciate what really happens in the liturgy because of halfhearted efforts. Parish leaders need to ask which liturgies best meet parishioners' needs, knowing that these vary greatly in every parish.

In reflecting on the role of liturgy in faith formation, *Sons and Daughters of the Light* says, "Liturgy is a key concern of young adults and is a primary meeting point with the Church. The quality of church life is often reflected in the prayerfulness and quality of its liturgy, which can be a connecting point between faith and life" (p. 35).

Parishioners' prayer needs sometimes differ from those who prepare the liturgies. Generally, people desire liturgies that are structured enough to enable them to appreciate what is happening and spontaneous enough to avoid the overformalized rituals that mean little to the average person. For example, some liturgists may put heavy stress on how high to hold the Bible when in procession or how to present the consecrated species to the people during the eucharistic prayer. Such issues have little impact on most people. It is better to examine such issues as "How can liturgy address real-life situations of the faithful?" Parishioners' actual needs are more important than quibbling over liturgical words or gestures.

Effective liturgy complements catechesis, witnessed in any successful RCIA program. When done well, the RCIA is a powerful experience of "being church." Although primarily a liturgical action, it includes an important catechetical component, which takes its departure from Sunday readings.

Catechumens need a systematic catechetical component that goes beyond reflections on the Sunday readings. This focuses on conveying basic church teaching in its entirety. Supplementary guides based on the liturgical year offer ways to expand lectionary-based catechesis. Church fathers like Ambrose, Basil, and John Chrysostom teach us this lesson. They employed a methodology, closely mirrored by our RCIA, in which they used auxiliary tests, sometimes resembling small catechisms, to supplement catechesis from liturgical books (Robert J. Hater, "Facilitating Conversion Processes," *Christian Adulthood,* USCC Printing Office, Washington, DC, 1987, pp. 11–12).

Effective liturgy leads to a desire for more catechesis, just as good catechesis prepares for liturgical celebrations. Both are different aspects of the same evangelization process. The complimentarity of catechesis and liturgy is illustrated in a simple way by parishes that provide a liturgy of the Word for children during one of the Sunday Masses.

## Ministry of Service

The ministry of service is the Christian response to Jesus' call to evangelize. Service is multifaceted. It includes creating a loving family environment and hospitable parish, assisting needy neighbors, and responding to society's hurts. Like catechesis and liturgy, service has informal and systematic aspects. Informally, Christian service spontaneously addresses personal, church, work, or social needs when they arise. Formally, it embraces organized parish activities, like a St. Vincent de Paul Society, soup kitchens, parish crisis teams, the Daughters of Charity, and the Legion of Mary. As *Sharing Catholic Social Teaching* says, "Catholic social teaching is a central and essential element of our faith" (p. 1). Some parish groups deliver food and clothing to the poor in Mexico or in a poor area of the community. Other parishioners make a commitment to help at a homeless shelter or Catholic Worker house.

Individuals can serve in many ways. Jim, a high school sophomore, assists in a nursing home, whereas Sally, an older adult, works at a woman's support shelter. Service activities include volunteer or paid positions. Counselors, teachers, doctors, and nurses exercise their professions in the spirit of the gospels, whereas engineers, corporate executives, or janitors further God's kingdom through just and compassionate decisions and lifestyles. Any job or activity motivated by God's love fulfills a Christian's responsibility to serve. Pedro, an office manager, invites his workers to pray with him if they come to him with a problem or disturbing news. The personal satisfaction that people receive from such service deepens their faith and praises God for their gifts.

Another critical area of service involves those committed to systemic change. Unjust social structures hold many people in poverty. Corporate officials, workers, union representatives, church workers, and parishes are challenged to expend strong efforts in changing unjust social structures, wherever they exist. Today's world needs people who give direct service to the poor as well as those who work to change the systems that keep people in poverty.

In an ecclesial context, a parish serves its members through its ministries. After Vatican II, specific ministries developed to meet community needs. These include religious education, sacramental preparation sessions, and ministries to divorced or elderly people. Some parishes, sensitive to the need for systemic change, sponsor programs to help people with community organizing, aimed at social justice.

While maintaining existing ministries, parish evangelization requires another element, which focuses ministerial efforts on people's key life moments. These include rites of passage, such as being baptized, entering a Catholic school, receiving first communion, obtaining a driver's license, graduating from high school, and leaving for college. These are occasions for leading people to deeper levels of faith and prayer. The same applies in times of joy or sorrow, such as marriage, divorce, sickness, and death. A vibrant parish vision recognizes such life moments as important opportunities to evangelize.

Parish leaders are encouraged to remind families, neighborhoods, and parish ministries of the many opportunities they have to show God's kingdom in action. When parishes organize their existing programs and ministries around such life experiences, evangelization relates to peoples' real needs.

## Management

*Management* is the fourth pillar of the parish. In Jesus' lifetime, certain apostles accepted responsibility for managing the purse strings and arranging for celebrations like Passover. The Acts of the Apostles and Paul's letters contain descriptions of organizational responsibilities in the early Church.

In like fashion, management serves an important function in every parish. As a ministry, it also needs to be energized by evangelization. This ministry involves leadership, organization, and planning. The leadership style involved in management differs from yet complements that required for pastoral counseling or liturgical ministry. Intended to further God's kingdom in the parish, effective management is critically important. Without it, parish ministry remains random, often unable to meet people's needs.

Effective parish management begins with a pastor who calls forth the community's gifts. Working with the pastor, the parish staff responds to parishioners' needs. Of particular importance in this endeavor are the lay professional ministers, including the pastoral, pastoral associate, and support staff. Lay volunteers, working with the ministerial staff, also play a critical role. In addition, the parish secretaries have a special place in administration. One pastor said, "The secretaries have the most control of day-to-day happenings in the parish, next to the pastor. Often they have the best feel for what is going on in the parish."

A staff's organizational acumen extends to its committees and organizations, including the parish or pastoral council, education commission, finance council or committee, and worship commission. All pastoral ministers need to make a commitment to a common vision, energized by Jesus' kingdom message. Otherwise, ministry degenerates into competitive bickering and superficiality.

A parish's organization puts flesh and bones on its vision of an evangelizing parish. Specific ministries organize the personnel, programs, and processes necessary to bring it to fruition. In one parish, this may mean hiring a professional leader to develop catechetical activities or liturgical celebrations; in another, this means hiring a minister to serve older adults; in still another, a person to facilitate youth ministry.

Large parishes require trained, professional staffs to deal with organizational demands and complex responsibilities. This means hiring ministers with the knowledge, skills, and temperament to organize specific ministries, collaborate with other parish ministers, and call forth volunteer ministers to meet catechetical, liturgical, and service needs. Small parishes may need a part-time, professional person to oversee ministry or may minister effectively with all volunteers. Effective parishes employ sufficient ministers to respond to peoples' needs.

St. Mark's Parish has a well-developed mission statement and enthusiastic members, but its management system falls short. It is not as effective as a similar parish, whose management system is better organized.

Whether professional or volunteer, ministers set the tone for a parish's evangelizing vision, based on the four pillars of mission, members, ministry, and management. A mission statement can focus parish priorities, ministries, organizations, and activities. The pastor, parish administrator, other ministerial staff members, and volunteers are responsible to develop and implement a parish's mission and ministries.

*Parish Life in the United States* illustrates the importance of competent staffs and organization. In studying successful parishes, it concludes that a parish's effectiveness does not depend on its "size, locale, language, income or presence of a school." Rather, it depends on the "way these parishes have structured their life and ministry" (*Parish Life in the United States,* USCC Printing Office, Washington, DC, 1983, p. 17). This finding reinforces the conclusion that each parish needs an adequate staff and organizational structure to deliver God's message.

All organized ministries carry out the ministries of Word, worship, and service. These include Catholic schools, parish schools of religion, adult catechesis, prayer groups, and youth ministry. Their success depends on leadership, organization, finances, and the ability of each specific ministry to relate God's kingdom message to parish needs. These might include counseling services, a food bank, or youth work.

## Pastoral or Parish Council

The *Code of Canon Law* discusses the issue of setting up a pastoral council in every parish (Can. 536, #1). Most U.S. parishes have one, sometimes called a "parish council." With its members selected from a cross-section of the parish, it offers a barometer of what happens in the parish and neighborhood. An effective pastoral council employs committees and subcommittees to supplement its work.

Not all pastoral councils have the same focus. At St. Francis Parish it is primarily a visionary body, composed of creative and insightful people who have their finger on the pulse of the neighborhood, parish, and broader Church. They leave more functional parish issues and ministerial procedures to other parish ministries. St. Margaret's pastoral council, on the other hand, concentrates on the overall direction of the parish, flowing from its priorities established in the parish plan. A pastoral council is not an administrative body. When it gets too involved in day-to-day parish administration, problems occur. It can only recommend policies to the pastor and oversees their general implementation. In this process, various commissions, including the education commission, report to it.

In describing the role of a pastoral council, Fr. Mike, the pastor said, "Pastoral councils in our area are to be visionaries for the parish. They are *not* the clearinghouse for all administrative procedures that happen in a parish. That is the role of the parish administrator. The pastoral staff often is in the position to implement what the pastoral council recommends. The pastoral council, through a wide process of consultation and committees, develops the parish's pastoral plan. The pastoral staff as well as other parish organizations or committees of the pastoral council implement the plan."

### Finance Council or Committee

The *Code of Canon Law* requires that a finance council be established in every parish. The pastor of a large parish described the operation of his finance council. He said, "In my parish, finance council members approve the parish and school budgets, review on a regular basis the cash flow and how the budgets are being followed, audit the various bank accounts in the parish, and make recommendations to assure the fiscal stability of the parish." He goes on to state that they do not decide how money is to be spent but advise on the prudent management of what is spent. In this parish they may even make recommendations to augment the income or trim the expenses.

This pastor concludes by saying, "The pastor may not undertake any major capital or other spending projects without consulting the finance council. Utilizing the gifts of its parishioners, a pastor through the finance council can compensate for his own limitations in this area."

Another pastor said, "In our parish, the chief responsibility of the finance council is to call the people to gospel financial stewardship." His words remind parishes that the ministry of stewardship, overseen by the finance council, is intended to further God's kingdom, not to build lasting testimonies in brick and mortar. The church, rectory, school, and parish center are important, but only if they fulfill their role in praising God and serving God's people.

Finance council members are servants of God's kingdom. They minister by exercising responsible stewardship in light of the gospel, not the bottom line. Sometimes this can get mixed up by well-meaning people, illustrated in the following episode.

In a smaller parish, a finance council pressured the pastor to fire all paid ministers, including a secretary and janitor, to balance the budget. The council wanted an all-volunteer staff. If the pastor followed its advice, ministry in the parish would have collapsed. The pastor refused.

Unfortunately, finances sometimes dictate a parish's evangelizing ministry. Effective parishes base their ministry decisions on their mission and priorities, not on money.

Management is critical to effective ministry. It grows in importance as smaller parishes are consolidated into larger ones, or lay administrators take over pastoral roles in parishes with no resident priest. Every such parish needs to balance its mission within a flexible, structured management system.

A vibrant parish vision inspires faith, ministry, and leadership. Although its form varies from parish to parish, one constant remains. Its vision must center on Jesus' kingdom as it relates to specific parish needs, carried out by competent ministries, and managed by dedicated leaders. As this happens, the Spirit may call the community to refocus its parish mission. This happens by using the best personnel, skills, and techniques that the Church and broader society offers.

## Meetings

Meetings of various kinds are necessary for running a well-ordered parish. The finance council, parish council, education commission, liturgical commission, men's and women's organizations, and other parish organizations need meetings to function effectively. Well-planned and managed meetings can generate new vision, motivation, and ministry. The kind and number of meetings varies with the size and needs of the parish. Generally, larger parishes require more meetings to keep their ministries functioning in an efficient way.

With the increase of organizations and staffs, parishes need to periodically reexamine the number and quality of their meetings. If not, staff members and parishioners can become overburdened, especially if they feel the meetings are poorly organized or unnecessary. As one pastor said, "Too often, meetings replace real ministry."

Parish leaders need to look critically at what must be handled at meetings and what can be done by administrators or on the phone. People should be asked to attend meetings only if they are necessary and well prepared. Under the guise of planning, many busy adults are deprived of time with families and loved ones because of parish meetings that sometimes produce few results. Parishioners often experience frustration when the items discussed at a meeting are more properly staff or administrative concerns. Ministerial leaders need to reexamine the value of the meetings they ask parents, single people, and other volunteers to attend. Effective parishes strive to have excellent meetings, not asking people to attend them unless they are necessary, well prepared, and to the point.

In meetings, a clear distinction needs to be made between policy and administration. All parish organizations, including the parish council and finance council, are advisory. They recommend policies, which need the pastor's concurrence to become parish policies. Generally, the pastor, pastoral and administrative staff, Catholic school administrators, and other parish leaders are responsible to implement these policies.

## Pastoral Suggestions

- Establish a family day in the parish, stressing various ways families can evangelize each other. Show video clips of family prayer services, display books that teach families ways to pray, make available other Catholic books, and show the variety of home devotions that are possible.

- Arrange for discernment seminars to identify ministerial needs and ministers to serve them, as well as to call forth these ministries in the broader parish.

- Establish an effective time, talent, and stewardship committee to analyze what is presently happening and recommend future possibilities.

- Make available a library of books for families desiring to get more information on teaching religion to their children.

- Do a home visitation of all parishioners who have registered or gone through the RCIA during the previous year.

- Prepare a special welcome at the Masses during one Sunday of Advent and Lent for all new parishioners, including hospitality for them after one Sunday Mass.

- Review the parish budget annually, asking what the allocation of parish funds says about the parish's commitment to evangelization.

- Have a representative parish group inquire of other religious and social agencies in the area how they see the parish's outreach to the neighborhood.

- Invite representatives of the diocesan catechetical and liturgical offices to give their opinions of the state of parish catechesis and liturgy.

- Provide a *Catechism of the Catholic Church* for all new religion teachers.

- Make available in the vestibule of the church a list of the various possibilities for parishioners to volunteer for service ministries.

- Put students, especially college students, from the parish on an e-mail directory and once a month send them a greeting and key happenings in the parish.

- Do a periodic evaluation of the quality and number of meetings the parishioners are asked to attend.

- Analyze the parish's effectiveness in dealing with multilingual issues and multicultural challenges within a language group.

- Look into developing an Elizabeth Ministry for the parish.

Parishes stand at a crossroad. Technology provides new ways to share God's message as the planet becomes a global community, populated by various ethnic groups with unique talents and abilities. Under competent leadership, a dynamic parish looks beyond its boundaries, recognizes the needs of all God's people, and responds as Jesus did. As this happens, evangelization, the driving force of the ministries of Word, worship, and service, motivates parish efforts. Chapter Six continues the evangelizing thrust established in this chapter, as it considers parish catechetical ministry.

PART THREE

*Living Out the Vision—
Chief Aspects of
Evangelizing Ministry*

# 6.

# Catechetical Ministry

Jason was anxious as he walked into St. Elizabeth's Pastoral Center to find out more about the Catholic faith on the first night of the new RCIA class. At nineteen, he had no formal religious background. When the pastor welcomed everyone, Jason felt at home, but he soon became nervous again for he knew little about what was said. After the session was concluded, he met with Eileen, the catechumenal director, and told her that he knew little of what they discussed. Eileen asked, "We treated fundamental matters. I am curious what you did not understand." Apologetically, Jason replied, "When you spoke about Jesus, I did not know anything about him." Eileen replied, "You never heard of Jesus?" Jason answered, "I heard his name before but don't know much about him. I'd like to learn more about him and the Catholic Church."

As the sessions continued, Jason spoke many times to Eileen. On one occasion he told her, "I am disappointed that my parents never allowed me to have anything to do with religion. I missed something important. As a boy, I only went to church twice with my grandparents." At the Easter Vigil Jason was admitted into the Catholic Church. Afterward, he told Eileen, "My newfound faith, the RCIA group, and you have given me something that was missing in my life. I am grateful."

Eileen and the Catholic community provided a supportive environment that encouraged Jason to question and learn. Such a climate is vital in adult faith formation. *Our Hearts Were Burning Within Us (OHWB)* says, "To be effective ministers of adult faith formation we will first, like Jesus, join people in their daily concerns and walk side by side with them on the pathway of life. We will ask them questions and listen attentively as they speak of their joys, hopes, griefs, and anxieties" (pp. 2–3).

Many Catholics under the age of forty-five have rudimentary knowledge of their Catholic faith. Some received very incomplete religious instructions in their childhood. Even those who attended Catholic schools or catechetical classes may not know much because their teachers often had fuzzy notions about Catholic beliefs. Unimpressed with what they were learning, many dropped out of formal religious instruction before they reached secondary school.

Since such adults do not know what to teach their children, they often teach them nothing. First- and second-grade catechists have children in class who do not know about Jesus, pray as a family, attend Mass, or have visible religious symbols in their homes. Solid catechesis is needed to help them and addresses their needs. Its importance often surfaces when parents bring their children to be baptized. This is a fruitful time to catechize parents, many of whom are open to learn about their Catholic faith. On such occasions, it helps to remember that we "will share with them the living Word of God, which can touch their hearts and minds and unfold the deep meaning of their experience in the light of all that Jesus said and did" (*OHWB*, p. 3).

The *General Directory of Catechesis (GDC)* puts it another way: "Jesus Christ not only transmits the word of God: he *is* the Word of God....The Gospels, which narrate the life of Jesus, are central to the catechetical message" (#98). This chapter addresses catechesis in five parts, namely Focusing Parish Catechesis, Dimensions of Catechesis, Catechetical Personnel, and Pastoral Suggestions.

## Focusing Parish Catechesis

Catechesis is an aspect of the evangelization process, for "evangelization—which has the aim of bringing the Good News to the whole of humanity so that all may live by it—is a rich, complex, and dynamic reality, made up of elements, or one could say moments, that are essential and different from each other, and that must all be kept in view simultaneously. Catechesis is one of these moments—a very remarkable one—in the whole process of evangelization" (*Catechesis in Our Time,* 18). With this in mind, this section considers adults, families, youth, and children. It also considers work as well as liturgical and service ministries.

### *Adults, Family, Youth, and Children*

Catechesis is multifaceted, reaching into every segment of the parish. It includes ministry to adults, families, teenagers, and children.

#### Adults

Many parishes are child-centered. While children's catechesis is critical, contemporary catechetical documents emphasize the priority of adult catechesis. When catechesis influences adults, it also affects their children. This requires a refocusing of direction because "placing ongoing adult formation at the forefront of our catechetical planning and activity will mean real change in emphasis and priorities" (*OHWB,* p. 4).

An important principle for adult catechesis is contained in the words, "In the catechetical process, the recipient must be an active subject, conscious and co-responsible, and not merely a silent and passive recipient" (*GDC*, #167). Many adults have not had the opportunity to tell their stories and would like to do so. The experience of adults is the fertile ground where the Word of God is heard and fostered.

Parish catechists need to take into account the various groups to whom they minister. The *General Directory of Catechesis* describes some of these groups as (1) active and faithful Catholics desiring to grow in their faith, (2) baptized but inadequately catechized adults, (3) fallen-away Catholics, and (4) nonbaptized persons, candidates for the RCIA (#172). Addressing these groups "requires taking into account of their problems and experiences, their spiritual and cultural resources, with full respect to their differences..." (#173).

Catechesis presents the "Christian faith in its entirety, and in its authenticity, in accordance with the Church's understanding" (*GDC*, #175). The *General Directory* goes on to say that this includes helping adults learn to love the scriptures and stressing the importance of prayer. The tasks of adult catechesis are:

- to promote formation and development of life in the Risen Christ...
- to educate toward a correct evaluation of the socio-cultural changes of our societies in light of faith...
- to clarify current religious and moral questions...
- to clarify the relationship between temporal actions and ecclesial action...
- to develop the rational foundations of the faith...

- "to encourage adults to assume responsibility of the Church's mission and to be able to give Christian witness in society" (#175).

Effective parishes employ various modes of adult catechesis. Paramount among them is the catechesis for Christian initiation that is used in the RCIA. Parish renewal programs and missions can also be very effective. Special situations require focused or systematic catechesis. These situations may include the times of marriage, baptism, and the reception of other sacraments. Catechesis can take place also during rites of passage, like a driver's license, school proms, graduation, military service, divorce, sickness, and death. The *GDC* also mentions catechesis for leisure times and special ecclesial or social events (#176). Flexibility is required in parish faith formation given the current context of an adult's life, including the reality that many parents work long hours outside the home. Intergenerational catechesis and whole-community catechesis are bringing together various age groupings of the parish into a unified perspective.

Adult-centered catechesis presumes God's presence in a person's story. Rooted in evangelization, it relates the Christian story to a person's own story in such a way that it invites the individual to new levels of integration, discovery, and response. No single model suffices for effective adult faith formation but all successful efforts appeal to adult needs and take their stories seriously. Since the most effective content for adult catechesis is the experience of the people involved, many adults respond well to these shared experiences. When adult catechesis includes their stories, they see better how God is present in their lives. Not all adults, however, respond positively to sharing their thoughts, attitudes, and feelings. If a shared-experience approach is employed with people not comfortable with this method, they may stop coming.

Adult faith formation often includes sessions during the day, businessperson's programs at work, lectures or workshops, retreats, and weekend renewal processes involving adult groups from parishes or schools. Such catechesis also needs to consider the situation of those who experienced divorce, death, or employment loss.

Young adults include a wide spectrum. They are "people in their late teens, twenties, and thirties; single, married, divorced, or widowed; and with or without children" (*Sons and Daughters of Light,* p. 7). Many of them have little knowledge of the Catholic faith and search for a religion that makes sense to them. Being very busy, they often do not respond to parish initiatives unless they are personally invited. Many do not frequent parishes where they find few inspiring liturgies. They search for spiritual connection, sometimes worshipping or enjoying fellowship in more welcoming churches.

The needs of frail and healthy older adults are at the other end of the spectrum. Many parishes offer programs for healthy older adults centering on social functions, like playing cards, social events, and outings. The pastor of a large metropolitan parish said, "One of our most active groups is 'Young at Heart.' These seniors love to go on day trips to religious spots for entertainment." There are many other good ways to gather them to have fun, offer spiritual advice, or engage in days of prayer, bible study, or recollection.

Older people ask a different set of questions than younger ones, and many of their spiritual needs go unmet. These needs range from how to deal with sickness and death to how to respond to anxiety over their children's leaving the Catholic faith. It is important to minister to older adults in their homes and retirement centers as the elderly population grows.

## Families

People discover God's presence through their family, friends, neighbors, and work associates. Parish catechesis does not share Jesus' message devoid of God's prior communication, but clarifies the God who is already present through scripture, Church teaching, and the witness of the Christian life.

Since catechesis exists to form Christian disciples, it "must often concern itself not only with nourishing and teaching the faith, but also with arousing it unceasingly with the help of grace, with opening the heart, with converting, and with preparing total adherence to Jesus Christ on the part of those who are still on the threshold of faith" (CT, 19). In this effort, catechesis is directed to the family and work place.

Families are the most important communities where catechesis happens, for God is uniquely manifested here. The family cannot be considered as "out there," like an "object" to be catechized. Rather, parish catechesis reinforces, supports, and builds on the faith initiated in family living. To see the family as the place where catechesis first happens invites parishes to emphasize the family's role in catechetical activities.

Parents are the primary catechists of their children. Such catechesis begins at birth and flows from the natural dealings of parents and children. Children learn religious values almost by osmosis. The Christian home climate itself educates with its practices and sacramentals, such as a crucifix, rosary, lives of the saints, Marian devotion, Advent wreath, family prayer, and a Bible. Family rituals, like prayer at meals and Sunday Mass attendance, set the tone for catechesis.

The influence of early religious practices is evident in Sam's story. He was a devout Catholic from birth. A stroke paralyzed him in his midyears. As he neared death, he slipped into a coma, and Edna, his wife, called Father Smith, the pastor. As he arrived at their home, she told him, "Sam will not be able to receive the Eucharist for he has lapsed into a coma and responds to nothing." Father Smith invited the family to receive communion for him. As Edna and her children gathered around Sam's bed, Father Smith anointed him and began the prayers before communion. When he said, "Let's say the Our Father for your Dad" and the family began the Lord's Prayer, Sam opened his eyes, smiled, and prayed with them. Conscious and alert now, he received communion. After the ceremony, Sam laughed and spoke with his family. Then he closed his eyes and fell back into the coma. Sam died the next day, never again regaining consciousness.

Afterward, Father Smith said he felt that when the family began the Our Father, early memories of saying this prayer triggered Sam's return to consciousness for the few moments when he received communion and spoke to his family.

A loving, forgiving home evangelizes children. Here people learn simple Christian beliefs about God, Jesus, and Mary, and practices of prayer, devotions, compassion, and forgiveness.

## Youth

Adolescents learn the Christian message according to their age and ability to comprehend it. Many youth have a deep spiritual hunger but do not appreciate the sacraments, Mass, and Christian moral values.

When interviewed, Beth, a youth minister at St. Andrew Parish's successful youth ministry program said, "The youth minister plays a vital role. This person must respect young people and help them grow spiritually, emotionally, and socially. For this to happen, the parish needs to provide sufficient money to develop multiple youth activities. The key ingredients of our youth ministry program include a balance between the social, service, and systematic catechetical aspects. All these are necessary for effective youth ministry."

Beth continued, "Teenagers need the *social* to provide fun, entertainment, sports, and other recreational activities. The *service* dimension meets their altruistic desire to help needy or aged people. Finally, and most importantly, the *systematic catechetical* component links God's Word and the other two components to their lives."

Teenagers flock to St. Andrew's youth ministry offerings where energy and enthusiasm abound. It carries out the three goals of ministry with adolescents indicated in *Renewing the Vision: A Framework for Catholic Youth Ministry*. These are "to empower young people to live as disciples of Jesus Christ in our world today...to draw young people to responsible participation in the life, mission, and work of the Catholic faith community...[and to] foster the total personal and spiritual growth of each young person" (pp. 9–18).

Besides sharing their common experiences, young people need good content sessions that teach basic Catholic doctrine, scripture, morality, and social justice. They need to learn the basics of the Catholic message and to appreciate the meaning of Catholic rituals like the Mass, Rosary, and sacraments. Such catechesis can effectively employ Internet offerings, audiovisuals, television programs, stories, and guided readings. The goal of adolescent catechesis is ongoing conversion to the Lord and a deeper appreciation of the Catholic faith.

Many youth are eager to help others, manifested in those who volunteer for projects like Habitat for Humanity. Many Catholic and Protestant youth groups conduct missionary trips, where young people spend time helping in poorer areas of the country. St. Charles Parish acknowledges and blesses their teenage youth group and their chaperones at Sunday Mass before they leave on their missionary endeavors. On such trips the young people's volunteer work is connected by the group leader to scripture readings and everyday life in ways that teenagers can understand. If such opportunities do not exist in Catholic parishes, Catholic teenagers may accompany Protestant youth groups and continue to worship with them when they return.

Effective youth ministry is connected with the broader parish. Some parishes encourage young people to take an active part in visiting retirement homes, providing entertainment, and praying for those who live there. This gives teenagers a concrete experience of Christian discipleship and enables them to reflect on God's Word and Church teaching in light of their experiences.

Any teenage activity, even sports, offers the occasion for spiritual growth. This can happen when coaches speak to young people about teamwork, Christian example, forgiveness, and defeat. Praying before a game, going on a day of reflection, or attending Mass together are ways to connect athletic events with faith. Something similar may apply at teenage outings, where prayer or bible reading is included during the event. Beth, the youth minister mentioned above, begins her youth outings with a reminder of God's presence in the activities they will do that day. Once, her youth group planned an overnight camping trip. After a fun-filled day of hiking, grilling out, and singing campfire songs, the young people fell silent as the coals of the fire vanished and stars appeared in a huge canopy in the heavens. Then a youth said, "The heavens proclaim the glory of God." After a long pause, they gathered in a circle, spoke of God's splendor, and expressed their gratitude. It was a wonderful example of cat-echesis in action, as young people and adult ministers reflected on God's Word.

Youth catechesis presents the Christian message in such a way that teenagers learn who Jesus is and what the Church teaches. It challenges them to live good lives and celebrate their faith in prayer and liturgy. This involves reading, study, prayer, liturgical and social response, and hard work for the youth and catechists alike.

## Children

Parents provide the key to effective catechesis. A child's early formative years are a fertile ground in which to plant the seed of Catholic faith, and parents till the soil from the very beginning. Since what is important for parents is also important for children, a father and mother profoundly impact their children through the testimony of their lives.

In a faith-filled family, children learn rituals of faith and simple Catholic teachings. This is illustrated by Dominic's story. His family prepared for Easter through prayer and scripture reading, and by putting up a crucifix in the family room. During Lent, his mother taught him that Jesus died for love of us. One afternoon, Dominic proudly showed his mother his hand-drawn picture of Jesus on the cross. Jesus was struggling, and his feet, head, and side were bloody. At the foot of the cross there stood a sad-looking man and woman. Dominic's mother said, "You have Mary and John at the foot of the cross. Firmly, Dominic said, "No, that's St. Joseph and Mary." In time, the boy will learn that Joseph was not there. Whether it was John or Joseph at the foot of the cross was not as important to Dominic's religious development as the fact that he learned about God's love of us, revealed by Jesus' death on the cross.

Children are capable of learning more than many cate-chists teach them. Some catechists do not ask children to memorize prayers and learn basic Catholic truths like the Ten Commandments. Sometimes, they learn little scripture. One frustrated parent said, "I don't get it. My children's reli-gion books are so superficial. They are capable of learning more than the books present or the catechist teaches." While the Church stresses adult faith formation, children's catech-esis cannot be neglected.

When people approach a parish to be married, Church ministers can help them see the importance of establishing a faith-filled home, including their role in children's catechesis. This is reflected in the words, "Infancy and childhood, each understood according to its own peculiarities, are a time of primary socialization as well as of human and Christian edu-cation in the family, the school and the Church" (*GDC*, #178). The importance of parental practice of the faith inten-sifies when parents have their children baptized. Baptism is a key rite of passage that affords parishes a rich opportunity to evangelize parents in how to share their faith. As the Church tells us, "For various reasons today, rather more than in the past, the child demands full respect and help in its spiritual and human growth....Those who have given life to children and have enriched them with the gift of Baptism have the duty continually to nourish it" (*GDC*, #177).

## Work

Effective catechesis also helps people view work as an important aspect of their Christian vocation and encourages them to see God as their copartner. It acknowledges today's many pressures, which may include the need for two incomes, high-tech jobs, unemployment, social mobility, and lack of security. A survey at St. Vincent's Parish indicated that parishioners felt the parish did a good job on family programs for adults and children but provided little to help them cope with work pressures. As questionable moral issues challenge them at work, Catholics often need assistance in deciding the right thing to do. These may include the morality of certain medical procedures, business decisions, and social involvement. By echoing Jesus' message, catechesis challenges Christians to say "No" to issues that are not of the Spirit. Such issues can be addressed in homilies, catechetical sessions, support groups, and enrichment programs.

## Liturgical and Service Ministries

Catechesis acts in partnership with liturgical ministries in sharing Jesus' evangelizing ministry. "From its earliest days, the Church has recognized that liturgy and catechesis support each other. Prayer and the sacraments call for informed participants; fruitful participation in catechesis calls for the spiritual enrichment that comes from liturgical participation" (*Sharing the Light of Faith*, #36).

Catechesis encourages a genuine liturgical participation, for "...catechesis, along with promoting a knowledge of the meaning of the liturgy and the sacraments, must also educate the disciples of Jesus Christian 'for prayer, for thanksgiving, for repentance, for praying with confidence, for community spirit, for understanding correctly the meaning of the creeds...'" (*GDC*, #85).

Parish catechesis is also related closely to the ministry of service. The *General Directory for Catechesis* connects Jesus, serving others, and the justice of God. It brings justice to the center of Jesus' message and holds Christians responsible for its proclamation, because the "proclamation of this judgment...is a central element of the Gospel, and Good News for the world: for those who suffer the denial of justice and for those who struggle to reinstate it; for those who have known love and existence of solidarity..." (#102). Justice has been a recurrent theme in papal encyclicals and other Church documents during the past two centuries. It was reiterated at Vatican II, the first Synod of Bishops after the council, and in many subsequent Church teachings.

Responsibility for catechesis belongs to the entire parish. Solid catechetical ministry happens when all parish ministries serve the one mission of Christ. Catechetical personnel monitor catechesis by concentrating on systematic catechesis, which employs the catechetical process.

## Dimensions of Catechesis

This section looks at *informal* and *systematic catechesis* and the *catechetical process.*

### Informal Catechesis

Informal catechesis happens all the time in a Christian home environment, as reflected in my experience with the Frank family.

As I rounded the corner and saw the Frank home, Susie, a six-year-old girl, waved both arms at me. Next to her stood Jill and Mark, her parents, and Noah, her younger brother. When they welcomed me into their home, I noticed a beautiful picture of Jesus, which hung between the living and dining rooms. After getting a tour of their house, we sat down to eat dinner and prayed. After dinner we played in the backyard.

The Frank family really enjoys each other's company. They pray together and make God the center of their home.

Each Sunday at Mass, the Franks sit near the front of the church. Their attention and enthusiasm witness to their deep faith. They integrate Sunday worship with faith in their home.

Regardless of family background or configuration, or socioeconomic class, the family creates an environment where God's Word thrives or withers. Faith in the home is the most important factor affecting both informal and systematic catechesis. Children learn about God in the religious atmosphere that parents create, for the "home is a primary context for sharing, celebrating, and living the Catholic faith..." (*Renewing the Vision,* p. 21). Parents teach their children about God through their love, positive attitude, good example, prayers, and forgiveness.

Informal family catechesis is an essential part of the Church's pastoral activity. A family environment of hospitality, prayer, religious pictures, crucifix, and stories of the saints sets the stage for what happens in parishes. Such an atmosphere is complemented by the hospitality and spirituality that a family finds when it attends Mass and parish functions. Such a climate informally catechizes children and adults while providing a receptive climate for systematic catechesis.

## *Systematic Catechesis*

Systematic catechesis includes those pastoral activities that call forth a response to the living Word of God in deliberate, intentional, and structured ways. Pope John Paul II describes the aim of systematic catechesis as a "matter of growth, at the level of knowledge and in life, to the seed of faith sown by the Holy Spirit with the initial proclamation and effectively transmitted by baptism" (*CT,* 20). Systematic catechesis addresses the whole person and invites the individual to change one's life through listening and responding to God's Word.

Parishes provide catechesis "so that the faith of the faithful becomes living, explicit, and productive through formation in doctrine and the experience of Christian living" (*Code of Canon Law,* #773). This canon complements those on Catholic education, which discusses parental responsibilities (#793), and indicates the Church's obligation to help people grow into the full Christian life (#794). Canon 795 stresses that such catechesis is holistic, developmental, social, and personal. All church educational systems are to carry out the basic orientation proposed in the canons that speak of catechesis and Catholic education.

Catechesis is a process that invites a person to hear, understand, interiorize, and respond to God's Word in acts of service and celebration. It simultaneously strengthens individual faith and deepens involvement in the community. If either of these is lacking, catechesis does not accomplish its full purpose. Catechesis is related to the broader process of incorporation into the Christian community. The *General Directory for Catechesis* says, "Primary proclamation is addressed to nonbelievers and those living in religious indifference. Its functions are to proclaim the Gospel and to call to conversion. Catechesis as 'distinct from the primary proclamation of the Gospel' promotes and matures initial conversion, educates the convert in the faith and incorporates him into the Christian community" (*GDC,* #61).

Catechesis helps families and parishes to respond to the living Lord whose presence is discerned in individual and communal experiences in light of the scriptures and in solidarity with the believing Church. The content of catechesis is the lived reality of the risen Lord, as he discloses himself to Christians. As John Paul II says, catechesis "aims therefore at developing understanding of the mystery of Christ in light of God's word..." (*CT,* 20).

A complimentary relationship exists between catechesis and religious instruction in Catholic schools. Religious instruction "is called to penetrate a particular area of culture and to relate with other areas of knowledge....It makes present the Gospel in a personal process of cultural, systematic and critical assimilation" (*GDC,* #73). Such instruction is an important dimension of the evangelization process.

Systematic catechesis employs a definite methodology and aims at presenting the entirety of the Christian message in an orderly and sequential manner. This can happen in the parish and in the home. Pope John Paul II alludes to systematic catechesis when he states, "Catechesis is an education of children, young people, and adults in the faith, which includes especially the teaching of Christian doctrine imparted, generally speaking, in an organic and systematic way, with a view to initiating the hearers into the fullness of Christian life" (*CT,* 21). Systematic catechesis builds on informal catechesis, or the many ways that God's Word indirectly touches a person. Systematic catechesis has "the twofold objective of maturing the initial faith and of educating the true disciple of Christ by means of a deeper and more systematic knowledge of the person and message of our Lord Jesus Christ" (C T, 19). Thus, two important elements summarize the specific character of systematic catechesis. First, it is didactic, concerned about teaching the Word to those ready to listen. Second, it aims at helping God's Word mature in the minds and hearts of those being catechized.

## The Catechetical Process

The following elements, which the catechetical process employs, are part of all systematic catechesis. Even though good catechesis employs widely differing methods, each one in some way includes the elements of *message, experience, integration,* and *response.*

Catechesis addresses the Christian *message* in the context of the life *experience* of those being catechized. It takes into account the individual's journey of faith, present needs, past experiences, and future aspirations, which it utilizes as the basis for listening to and responding to God's Word in light of the teachings of Jesus and the Church. This dimension of the catechetical process aims at teaching and being informative. It emphasizes the content of the Catholic faith and includes memorization of basic facts and prayers.

*Integration* leads the person to reflect on and internalize the message by seeing how it can change one's life. It helps the person realize the implications of what is presented. Finally, the catechetical process invites one to *respond* to God's Word in action. It asks for an honest response to what has been learned, which leads to acts of service and worship. The catechetical process with ongoing conversion as its goal centers around God's revealed message as it addresses life and invites one to change.

Parish catechesis is everyone's responsibility. The *General Directory for Catechesis* sums up the ecclesial nature of catechesis by saying, "Catechesis is nothing other than the process of transmitting the Gospel, as the Christian community has received it, understands it, celebrates it lives it and communicates it in many ways" (#105).

## Catechetical Personnel

The pastor, catechetical leaders, school principal, and catechists are keys to successful parish catechesis. Each has special roles, responsibilities, and opportunities. Their collaborative efforts enhance parish catechetical ministry.

### Pastor

The pastor is the chief catechetical leader in a parish (*Catechism of the Catholic Church*, §757). He is a servant of the Word through his preaching, overseeing parish catechetical instruction, fostering the spirit of the gospels, and providing an open climate for catechesis. The *Code of Canon Law* emphasizes the pastor's responsibility for all pastoral ministries, including systematic catechesis (canon 515). The pastor guides the gifts of other catechetical ministers as they nourish parish catechetical life.

The responsibility of the pastor for catechesis is reaffirmed in the words, "Conscious, on the other hand, that their ministerial Priesthood is at the service of 'the common Priesthood of all the faithful,' priests foster the vocation and work of catechists and assist them in carrying out a function which springs from Baptism and is exercised in virtue of a mission entrusted to them by the Church" (*GDC*, #224). The pastor influences the shaping parish catechesis, its quality, and the type of ministers selected as catechetical leaders and catechists. He is responsible for seeing that catechetical leaders are qualified. They, in turn, see to catechist formation, which is the most important aspect of successful parish catechesis.

### Catechetical Leaders and School Principals

While the revised *Code* emphasizes the pastor's responsibility for catechesis, it also advises him to enlist others to share in this ministry. Catechetical leaders can be full- or part-time, paid or volunteer, directors or coordinators of religious education and catechesis in a parish or school setting. They assist parish catechists and Catholic school catechetical ministers. The success of catechetical ministry depends largely upon them. Their responsibilities are many and varied, focusing on creating a climate for effective catechesis and working with the pastor and liturgical and service ministers. Their tasks include screening and training catechists; establishing and maintaining a resource library; screening and recommending audio, visual, and technological resources; selecting textbooks; and monitoring new catechetical possibilities on the Internet and in the diocese.

Catholic school principals are our schools' ministerial leaders. Some are also catechetical leaders. Their responsibility for catechesis varies, but in every instance the principal exercises a supervisory role in all catechetical activities, seeing to it that school catechesis is excellent, complete, and in harmony with the broader parish catechetical vision.

## Catechists

The catechist's ministry involves a response to the Lord's call as articulated by the parish. This call invites a person to give one's talent and time to catechize others and to help them grow in faith and understanding. In this ministry, the "catechist is essentially a mediator. He facilitates communication between God and people and the mystery of God, between subjects amongst themselves, as well as with the community" (*GDC*, #156).

Catechetical formation is necessary to improve the quality of parish catechesis. Hence, motivating and training catechists is a top priority of effective parishes. They concentrate on catechist preparation as being the key to effective parish catechesis. Parishes that take catechist formation seriously have better prepared and more confident catechists. There is much less turnover because catechists have made an investment of their time and take pride in what they do. When catechists are vibrant, creative, and knowledgeable, with the faith and skills to communicate the Christian message, catechesis bears fruit. The opposite happens if catechists are poorly prepared.

Catechetical preparation is necessary to serve God's people. It includes growing in faith, learning basic Church teachings, and developing catechetical skills. All catechists need to participate in workshops, seminars, and courses, as well as to read books, journals, and other literature that contribute to their ongoing spiritual, catechetical, and theological enrichment.

When a parish has well-trained catechists, other catechetical needs take care of themselves. Without adequately prepared catechists, even the best topics of study, curriculum guidelines, books, media, or evaluative tools are not very effective. An excellent book in the hands of a poor catechist will never accomplish what an excellent catechist can do, regardless of the book. It is better to take the time to prepare catechists than to offer catechetical sessions with ill-prepared teachers.

Effective catechetical programs connect with the parish vision for evangelization and do frequent evaluations of their courses, leaders, and catechists. The time has come for parishes to take evaluation more seriously. The ultimate test of catechetical effectiveness is the outcome on those being catechized. Parishes want to know, "How much did those being catechized learn?" Evaluation and testing is a good place to begin.

## Pastoral Suggestions

To insure the continued effectiveness of catechetical ministry the following are suggested:

- Ask the education commission to do a comprehensive evaluation of the parish catechetical program on an annual basis, using an instrument provided by the diocesan catechetical office.

- Include in the above, an evaluation of catechetical leaders, catechists, school principal, and those being catechized.

- Use an evaluation tool for every parish catechetical session from early childhood to adult faith formation, making the catechist or facilitator responsible for this process.

- Include in the catechetical evaluation process a test given to those being catechized to learn whether they have learned their memorized prayers, the commandments, and other significant aspects of the faith.

- On a semi-annual basis, ask the catechetical leader to compile the results of such evaluations and submit them to the pastoral council or education commission.

- Require that all parish catechetical leaders and catechists have a diocesan certificate or are in the process of obtaining one before they begin to catechize.

- Pay for all the courses or workshops required for catechetical certification.

- Have the catechetical leader do a periodic evaluation of the textbooks used in the religious education program and report the results to the education commission.

- Ask the school principal and the catechetical leader to do a joint retreat for the children making their first communion or being confirmed as well as a joint service project for elementary or junior-high-school age children in order to stress cooperation between the Catholic school and parish school of religion.

- Invite the youth director to investigate the effectiveness of other youth ministry programs.

- Ask the education commission and the pastoral council to establish a reasonable budget for catechetical materials, including books and audiovisuals.

- Have the appropriate minister arrange Sunday morning sessions for adult faith formation between or after the Masses during Lent, Advent, or other pertinent times, concentrating on scripture teaching and current interest areas for parents and other adults.

- Invite a staff member to select a committee to look into developing a parish intergenerational religious education program.

- Send parish representatives from the education commission to parishes that have a reputation for excellent catechetical parishes to see how they handle this ministry and what can be learned from their success.

- Ask for volunteers to develop a "Busy Person's Retreat" program at noon one day a week during Advent and Lent.

- During Advent, offer sessions on the "nativity accounts" of Matthew and Luke, presented by a competent scripture teacher, stressing the meaning of these stories and their applicability today. During Lent, do the same with the "passion narratives" from the four Gospels.

- During January or February, conduct a one-day seminar around the theme of "effective fathers and grandfathers."

- Ask the liturgical coordinator to arrange a seminar for family members in late fall, explaining various Catholic ritual practices, like the Advent wreath, Jesse Tree, and Kris Kindle, to be used for prayer and celebration in the home.

- Invite a group of Catholic schoolteachers and/or volunteer catechists to work with the children to plan an Advent fair, concentrating on Advent and Christmas traditions from other countries and cultures and inviting parishioners from these cultures to participate. Compile these traditions and send them home with the children before Christmas.

- Provide up-to-date catechetical materials for each catechetical program.

- Do a living nativity procession on the parish grounds the Sunday before Christmas.

- Sponsor twice-yearly youth retreats for teenagers and/or their parents.

- Once each season, ask the minister responsible for young adult ministry to invite the young adults to gather at the evening Mass on Saturday or Sunday, followed by an hour of meditation, reflection, music, and prayer in a relaxed parish setting.

- Have the catechetical leader look into setting up a Sunday morning intergenerational catechetical program focusing on young children.

- Identify a coordinator for young adult ministry if one is not in place.

- Invite the youth minister to investigate the success stories of neighboring Protestant church programs for young people and learn from what they do.

- Set up a catechetical fair around Catechetical Sunday, providing information on catechetical programs, inviting volunteers to serve in this ministry, and encouraging parents to focus on their role in their children's informal and systematic catechesis.

- Have the catechetical director make available in the Sunday bulletin some good religious resources available on the Internet.

- Ask a volunteer interested in catechesis to correspond weekly through e-mail with all those involved in parish religious education.

- Tape and/or transcribe Sunday homilies and make them available to parishioners and shut-ins.

- Establish a way for teenagers in catechetical programs to do volunteer service in the parish and beyond, especially with aged or needy people.

- Do a yearly assessment of the diverse catechetical needs of the parish.

- Let the parish's commitment to adult faith formation be reflected in the special care given to catechesis at times like marriage, divorce, death, and sickness.

- Balance the commitment to the parish school, if one exists, with the parish's financial responsibility to provide for other parish catechetical needs.

- Ask the parish ecumenical commission to investigate working with an area Protestant church to do joint programming in adult faith formation.
- Provide a semiannual day of recollection for senior citizens, centered around scripture.
- Pay fair salaries and benefits to professional catechetical personnel.
- Ask the parish catechetical leader to look into the feasibility of "whole-community catechesis" for the parish.

To regard the parish as a community of smaller communities that gather to hear and celebrate God's Word gives parish ministers the flexibility needed to catechize various parish segments. A well-articulated philosophy of catechesis encourages more effective ministry to all parishioners.

The parish proclaims Jesus' call to the kingdom by teaching God's Word. Catechetical ministry happens in families, parish outreach, Catholic schools, RCIA processes, adult enrichment, youth ministry, ministry to children, and a variety of other parish activities. To deepen their faith, while sharing hospitality or engaging in various parish events, parishioners need ongoing catechesis. Catechetical personnel enhance community faith growth by viewing the entire parish as the place where catechesis happens. What happens in catechesis is celebrated in the liturgy, which is discussed in Chapter Seven.

# *Liturgical Ministry*

Expectation filled the congregation as the Palm Sunday liturgy began. After the initial greeting, the ministers walked to the center of the people, and I blessed the palm.

The Gospel describing Jesus' entrance into Jerusalem mounted on a donkey reminded me of a painting of this scene by Benjamin Joseph Haydon (1786–1846), which hangs in the foyer of Mt. St. Mary's of the West Seminary, Cincinnati, Ohio. This life-sized painting shows a crowd that includes famous humanists, scientists, and artists of Haydon's time, like Wordsworth, Voltaire, Newton, and Keats. One legend says that Haydon painted his own face on Jesus' body. Another says he never got Jesus' face the way he wanted it. Many people meditating on this painting wonder why Jesus' light face contrasts so sharply with the darker faces of those in the crowd.

The glow radiating from Jesus speaks of something beyond the immediate scene depicted. Upon further reflection, one may conclude that Jesus' entrance into Jerusalem was not his alone, but every person's journey. Palm Sunday represents high points in our lives, like graduations, promotions, and birthdays. In Jesus' face, I see every faithful person, joyful at key life moments, but aware that such time will not last. This realization can cast an ambiguous tinge on the most joyful events.

When honored, we sometimes feel embarrassed because we know our imperfections and realize that a present reward is only a fleeting high point amidst life's joys and sorrows. Haydon's painting reminds me that the cross enters every person's life and that taking up our cross leads to eventual resurrection. Palm Sunday invites us to sit on the donkey with Jesus and to enter our own Jerusalem. Seeing ourselves there, it becomes clearer why Haydon depicted Jesus' face differently from the others in the scene. Jesus knows something about life that we can only strive to discover. The aura of mystery that Haydon captured in Jesus' face symbolizes our ambiguity during life's journey, which passes through Holy Thursday to Good Friday and on to Easter Sunday. The glow on Jesus' face bespeaks of the realization that more than this earth's joys and sorrows await us. Eventually, there will be no more tears and no more sorrow, for we will live forever in God' glory.

The Haydon painting also reminds us that we cannot superficially celebrate liturgy. It requires entrance into the mystery of God' love, revealed in the paschal mystery. The Church's liturgical year revolves around this mystery into which Holy Week initiates us. If we appreciate this great week, we better appreciate the liturgy. For liturgy to speak to our deep needs we must celebrate it at the core of who we are as humans and Christians. This chapter addresses the meaning and heart of liturgy and the rituals that celebrate it; it addresses the topic in four parts, namely, The Meaning of Liturgy, Challenges to Liturgy, Enhancing Parish Liturgy, and Pastoral Suggestions.

## The Meaning of Liturgy

All liturgical actions make present the ongoing fulfillment of the paschal mystery as it continues in the Christian community. Since the Lord lives among us, the graces he gained on the cross are perpetually showered on his people. Entrance into this mystery begins in baptism, is celebrated at each Eucharist, and is strengthened in the other sacraments.

Liturgy, a form of ritualistic action, is one element or moment in the evangelization process. Christian rituals celebrating the life of faith revolve around the paschal mystery. Within the Christian community God offers us the salvation merited by Jesus Christ. Seen in this way, Christian liturgy is the communal celebration of the ongoing dying and rising of Jesus by people called together in the Spirit to remember the continued gift of God's love, to engage in repeatable ritualistic action commemorating the paschal mystery, and to respond in service to the permanent reality of God's Spirit.

All liturgies acknowledge God's self-manifestation and the community's response in prayer, but not all liturgical celebrations have the same degree of intensity. The chief liturgical actions are public communal faith responses to the paschal mystery by the Christian community. The history and wisdom of the community dictates the form these liturgical activities take, which include the centrality of the eucharistic liturgy, the seven sacraments or mysteries of the Christian life, and the Liturgy of the Hours. These focus their dynamism through the yearly liturgical cycle. As public manifestations of the Church's fullness, they use official liturgical rites, and designated ministers preside over them.

Family prayer, certain public devotions, and other communal prayers celebrate the paschal mystery in a less comprehensive way. Sometimes we refer to these devotions, even if performed in communal gatherings, as "private" devotions. They deepen the Christian faith by supplementing official liturgical actions. Many Catholics rely on private devotions like the Rosary, other Marian prayers, and devotions to the saints to enhance their faith. As Harriet, an older Catholic, said, "I need more spiritual input than weekly Mass provides me. The Rosary and private prayers fill this need." As long as private devotions supplement, but do not replace, official Church rituals, they serve an important role in Catholic life. Regardless of their form, they have the paschal mystery as their ultimate focus, just as official liturgical actions do.

Private prayer sets the foundation for public prayer. Without private prayer, no foundation exists to sustain the Church's liturgy, which is the communal culmination of what private prayer seeks and anticipates. Parishes can develop fine liturgical celebrations, but if parishioners are not prepared for such liturgies through private and family prayers, they have limited impact. For this reason, effective parishes help people learn to meditate, pray with scripture, and engage in meaningful devotions. Such parishes realize that this present "generation of seekers" strives to discover ways to connect with deep life dimensions.

All liturgical action aims at deepening the realization of God's love and life's purpose. It needs to be particularly sensitive to people at key life moments, which is illustrated in the following story.

Father Gene, pastor of an inner-city parish, learned about Isaac, a retired musician, from another parishioner. For thirty-eight years he entertained thousands of admiring fans with his trumpet-comedy act as he traveled from city to city. The music world admired him as a good, competent man. Eventually, when age caught up with him, Isaac stopped travelling. In his latter years he barely had enough money to live on.

When Father Gene first visited him, Isaac played his trumpet and gave the priest a taste of his skills as a comedian. Several months later he could play no longer. Father

Gene anointed Isaac as he became weaker, and he died shortly afterward.

About seventy musician friends attended Isaac's Mass of Christian Burial. A silent reverence overcame the congregation during the liturgy even though most attendees were not Catholic. Father Gene's homily centered on Isaac's call to make audiences happy through his musical gifts. The priest reflected on how God blessed the wholesome comedy that Isaac provided for his audiences. After Mass, many attendees thanked the priest, speaking with tears in their eyes.

Their comments reflected the same theme, spoken by an older man who said, "This is the first time since my childhood that I felt welcome in a church. You made us feel that our musical efforts to make people happy were blessed by God." After he spoke, a younger woman replied, "I was a Catholic but left the Church years ago, because I felt I was not wanted. The stage became my church, but I never lost my faith in God. After listening to your homily I believe God wanted me to do what I have done these past years. I plan now to find a church that will welcome me." Father Gene touched the core dimension of these musician's lives.

## Dimensions of Meaning

To appreciate the dynamics occurring in the above liturgy, we consider the interconnected dimensions of *core, community,* and *secondary meaning.*

*Core dimension* refers to deep aspects of life where all people are alike. It speaks of our common joys and fears, including suffering and death. It moves us to ask why we were born, what life's meaning is, and what happens after death. It looks for connections with the earth and other humans, a sense of balance, and personal and group identity.

Catholic life, teaching, and practice address such issues within the context of the paschal mystery.

The *community dimension* involves ultimate life relationships, which begin in infancy and last until death. These include relationships with our parents, siblings, friends, spouses, colleagues, and neighbors. Early family relationships influence our attitudes toward basic life questions. In this regard, families and ethnic groups are especially significant.

Ritual patterns developed in faith-filled homes affect the way we address fundamental questions like those involving happiness, identity, and suffering. The community dimension influences where we put our priorities.

The *secondary dimension* is the realm of the functional, rational, and objective. Included here are the meanings we find in our computers, homes, automobiles, and money. These are important, but secondary. They cannot fully satisfy us even though many people treat them as life's ultimate goal.

In liturgical actions, secondary dimensions refer to everything that makes for a smoothly flowing liturgy, including liturgical preparation, rubrics, sanctuary arrangement, church climate, and the presider's style. These give directions for an efficient, well-ordered liturgy. While important, a church's size, the homily's length, music, liturgical vestments, lectionary position, and sanctuary's arrangements are secondary.

The *community dimension* includes the interactions of the worshipping congregation. The parish assembly, which celebrates the liturgy, connects with the Catholic community throughout the world. Every liturgical action reminds us that the Body of Christ is universal, transcending time and space.

To facilitate a prayerful community atmosphere, parishes need to be sensitive to their people. Such sensitivity creates a welcome climate and family spirit. Every parish hears God's Word and celebrates the Eucharist in the context of those assembled. For this reason, a liturgy's community and secondary dimensions must connect with the assembled people, so that the liturgical actions can touch core dimension of people's lives.

## Connecting at the Core

Liturgy's core dimension centers on celebrating the paschal mystery. Touching this core dimension is the goal of every liturgy. In the above story of Isaac's funeral liturgy, the communal welcome and Father Gene's homily touched this dimension. It began with the welcome to the mourners as the parish community invited them into a deeper experience of God. The congregation's prayerful listening to God's Word and the homily, which connected the Word with their experiences, prepared them to say "Amen" to the Lord's presence in the Isaac's life. Liturgy always touches the core when the Lord's presence is manifested in the community, proclaimed in the Word, celebrated in the Eucharist, and symbolized in the person, actions, and homily of the presider.

A liturgy's core dimension is multifaceted. Easter and Christmas celebrate the foundations of faith. Baptism, marriage, and funeral liturgies touch archetypal moments. At such times, the church's climate, music, and homily enhance a congregation's openness to God, who transcends the liturgy itself.

Any liturgical celebration throughout the year can connect with the core level. The key to doing so is not found in gimmicks or the right musical style. It goes deeper, since liturgical response is affected by the participant's faith. Community belief enhances individual faith and sets the stage for a loving acceptance of the Lord in Word and Sacrament.

Moving to the core at any celebration begins with welcome. This happens when those attending feel they belong there, especially important at key rites of passage in a person's life, like divorce. If this happens during the liturgy, a friend might encourage a divorcee to attend Mass even though the person may initially feel embarrassed, not knowing how the congregation might react.

A faith community moves to the core when the welcome, music, and homily connect with deep life dimensions and when the scriptures are proclaimed in ways that help us see God in our ordinary lives. In such instances, we are reminded that we work out our salvation in the everyday, not through occasional spectacular experiences.

We celebrate liturgical actions as a priestly people when the living Lord ministers through our worship, for all liturgy praises the indwelling, yet transcendent God. The liturgy celebrates the living God, because the community is the Body of Christ. Jesus' continued action in the liturgy makes it one action of head and members. The Risen Christ, as principal priest at every Mass, offers one eternal act of praise to the Father. (See John Paul II, *On the Eucharist.*)

Throughout Christian history the faithful have acknowledged the liturgy's transcendent dimensions. From the beginning Christians believed that Jesus' dying and rising continues through the Church's liturgical ministry. As they pondered this mystery, adherence to Church teaching insured faithfulness to fundamental Catholic belief. Medieval theologians spoke of the *ex opere operato* effects of the sacraments, which are those effects that flow from the liturgical action itself, independent of the style, external surroundings, or dispositions of the celebrant. This language goes to the core belief that whenever the community through a designated minister celebrates the liturgy, the Risen Lord is present. The dying and rising of Jesus continues at Mass even if an excommunicated priest presides. Baptism produces its effects even if a non-Christian nurse, intending to do what the Church does, baptizes an infant in an emergency situation because the parents requested it. The liturgy helps us experience the depths of God's love in a holistic way, which transcends our intellectual comprehension of how the Lord ministers through the sacraments.

The Church also has described the *ex opere operantis* effects of the sacraments, which are those effects influenced by the dispositions of the presider and participants in liturgical actions—a person's faith, moral worthiness, and present condition. These effects are enhanced by a moving eucharistic celebration, solid liturgical preparation, and effective preaching. Such liturgies help the community enter into the mystery of the Lord's love. Secondary dimensions of the liturgy, like the temperature in church or the presider's liturgical style, also increase our readiness to celebrate the Eucharist or other sacraments.

The liturgical year celebrates the saving acts of Christ's redemption and also remembers the saints so that we, like them, might follow the path of salvation wherever we are or whatever we do. Thus, our entire life becomes a reflection of the paschal mystery.

## Challenges to Liturgy

The fast pace of our generation influences everything we do. It creates excitement for the new, but its preoccupation with the superficial often leaves us searching for deeper meaning. This quest for more creates a generation of seekers, as economic, political, and social uncertainties remind us that change is just around the corner. This climate affects confidence in our neighborhoods, families, marriages, and Church. It also influences this generation of worshipping Catholics.

"The faithful" is an expression used since early Christian days to refer to committed Church members. The Rite of Christian Initiation of Adults distinguishes between "the catechumens" and "the faithful." The commitment implied by "the faithful," can no longer be presumed today. Even where such commitment exists, external forces challenge them. These challenges often lead to a generation of seekers, many of whom are baptized Catholics not seriously committed to the Lord or the Church.

Catholic liturgy generally presumes that the congregation consists of committed members of the faithful. Its primary focus is not directed toward the seeker. Considering the present state of Catholics, this needs to be reexamined. While the fundamentals of liturgy cannot change, many parishioners are seekers and the liturgy and ministers need to take into account the seeker dimension of their lives. The success of some fundamentalist oriented megachurches, meeting in auditorium-type spaces with soft chairs, attest to the seeking dimension present in the contemporary religious search. In one such church 65 percent of the congregation consists of former Catholics. This church presumes that its members are seekers and responds accordingly in liturgical celebrations, ministry outreach, and structures. Catholic parishes can learn something about this generation of seekers from such churches. Five suggestions are offered to enhance parish liturgies.

## 1. Appreciate the Reality of Today's Seeking Catholic

Wise parishes acknowledge the presence of both committed Catholics and seekers among their members. Recognition of these groups and the challenges each present is just the beginning of addressing this complex issue. The different needs of both groups can be considered by the parish council, liturgy or worship commission, and educational commission.

The phenomenon of the Catholic seeker applies across the board to young and old alike. People seek answers amidst the shifting sands of society. They go to spiritual directors or counselors, study scripture, attend Christian churches geared to seekers, do volunteer work with the poor, and participate in small sharing groups.

## 2. Acknowledge the Seeking Generation in All Liturgical Endeavors

While Catholic parishes can never develop the informal atmosphere that allows auditorium-like arrangements and coffee holders in the pews, the realization that a seeking generation makes up a significant part of the congregation helps parishes arrange more appropriate music and homilies. Successful Christian churches often blend uplifting music with solid preaching. The former connects the congregations with the world where they live and work; the latter gives them a stable message in a changing world.

A positive climate reinforces the self-worth of this generation of seekers. They get enough negative messages from society. They hunger to hear that God loves them and that they are to love one another. Seekers want to know they are welcome and important. They desire a community of support that is convinced of the faith that it professes. The energy within a prayerful, dynamic celebration moves seekers to conclude that their time spent in worship is worthwhile. Seekers also are pleased when hospitality follows the liturgy in an informal setting. That's the reason hospitality after Masses is more important than ever, providing opportunities for parishioners to meet new members and connect with their friends. Parishes might even consider leaving more time between Masses to provide greater flexibility for hospitality and to develop a communal spirit.

When reflecting on the environment needed to attract today's seekers, it helps to listen to Emily's experience. She is an active member of an Episcopalian church who brought her son to a large fundamentalist-type Christian church as part of an ecumenical endeavor. Later, Emily told a friend about their experience. She said, "Soon after Aaron and I arrived in the lobby, a church member escorted us to our theatre-style seats. After a few moments, Aaron examined a card that he picked up when we entered the church. After studying it, he signed the card, giving his name, address, and phone number. Curious as to what he was doing, I said. 'Aaron, what is that card?' He replied, 'An inquiry card inviting me to seek more information about this church.' I continued, 'What interests you about this church?' He said, 'It's the welcome and open atmosphere, Mom. The place is alive with the same spirit that I experienced at last summer's youth rally, when fifteen thousand young people traveled to Houston.'"

Emily then remarked to her friend, "As an active church member of the Episcopalian Church, I was scared by how quickly Aaron identified with what was going on in this church. The key is the seeker. What do we do to meet their needs? The welcome Aaron felt came from the environment of the entire congregation. They really made us feel at home and that we were wanted."

That's a challenge for Catholic parishes.

### 3. Provide Opportunities for Service Ministries

In the liturgy that Emily attended, the pastor stressed Christian service to the poor. After the service, Emily and Aaron spoke to a church member. The latter asked Emily if she would go with her to pray with poor people. "When?" Emily asked. "Right now," was the reply. Emily had never prayed with strangers so she asked, "Where are we going?" "To the projects," was the answer. Emily agreed to go and soon they were on the third floor of a building, knocking on doors and asking, "Do you need prayers today?" At the same time they gave every person a free light bulb with a note describing Jesus as the light of the world.

During their visits they knocked on one door, but no one answered. After exiting the building a woman called from the window of this room, "Church people, please come back, I did not know it was you. I need prayers today." The people waited for these visits with the prayers and free light bulb. When asked later, "How many people refused to allow you to pray with them," Emily responded, "No one."

This church committed its members to service of a spiritual kind. This service continued what the congregation heard from the church preacher and discussed afterward in a hospitality gathering with their small group.

The Catholic parish needs to frequently encourage the faithful to accept Jesus' call to serve the broken of the world. As John Paul II says in *The Vocation and Mission of the Lay Faithful,* "*You go too....*The call is addressed to everyone: lay people as well are personally called by the Lord, from whom they receive a mission on behalf of the Church and the world" (#2). Then he expands on the responsibility for Christian service: *"The 'world' thus becomes the place and the means for the lay faithful to fulfill their Christian vocation,* because the world itself is destined to glorify God the Father in Christ" (#15).

The parish also needs to remind the family that it is the first church anyone attends. The above quoted document says, "The *Christian family*, as the 'domestic Church,' also makes up a natural and fundamental school for formation in the faith…" (#62).

## 4. Commit the Parish to
## Extra-Liturgical Modes of Participation

Jeff, a middle-aged man, researched the reasons why a large, Christian congregation, composed of many former Catholics, is so popular. He said, "The congregation is composed largely of seekers, not satisfied with how the Catholic Church or mainline Protestant churches have spiritually fed them. This church's success begins in the liturgy but is attributable largely to number of small groups that the church nourishes. Over sixty ministers serve these groups. Here people search for core values in conjunction with other seekers by reflecting largely on the Word of God in Scripture."

Then Jeff continued, "What in the Catholic Church is comparable with the various support group ministries in this church? In the past, the Church encouraged small groups, like women's sodalities, men's societies, and Third Order of St. Francis groups. Today's small groups or Christian communities within a parish stress scripture. Efforts like "Renew" and "Christ Renews His Parish" give support and spiritual insights to those who attend. The latter is essential, for more needs to be done to meet the spiritual needs of today's seekers. The liturgy alone does not touch their core needs. They need more, which parishes are challenged to help them find."

The focus on small Christian communities centering on scripture is growing. Many adult faith formation programs use scripture as a basis for reflection, at least part of the time. This also happens in youth programs, which often find scripture study and prayer more effective than social activities to attract young people. As parishes continue to place more importance on scripture, new and more engaging ways to proclaim the Word of God are emerging.

## 5. Connect Liturgical Celebrations with Catechetical Ministry

The Rite of Christian Initiation of Adults clarifies the complementary roles of catechesis and liturgy. This also is emphasized in the statement, "The Church ardently desires that all the Christian faithful be brought to that full, conscious, and active participation which is required by the very nature of the liturgy and the dignity of the baptismal priesthood. For this reason, catechesis, along with promoting a knowledge of the meaning of the liturgy and sacraments, must also educate the disciples of Jesus Christ 'for prayer, for thanksgiving, for repentance, for praying with confidence, for community spirit, for understanding correctly the meaning of the creeds…,' as all of this is necessary for a true liturgical life" (GDC, #85).

The liturgy is the chief way that the community catechizes in Eastern Catholic Churches. They supplement this with religious instructions and other forms of catechesis. The Western Catholic Church has tended in the past to separate catechesis and liturgy, employing different methods for each.

This is changing as greater collaboration between liturgists and catechists occurs especially at the time of baptism, first communion, marriage, and the anointing of the sick.

## Enhancing Parish Liturgy

When a riot broke out in Cincinnati during Holy Week 2001, Catholic churches addressed the critical situation from the pulpit, in prayer, and through outreach to the needy. Acknowledging the tense situation allowed parishes to connect God's Word with what was happening. Parishioners experienced more fully the paschal mystery during Holy Week because it was connected with their lives.

Liturgy involves more than preparation, music, and rubrics. It requires more than a comfortable worship space, beautiful flower arrangements, or contemporary vestments. These enhance but never create a moving liturgy by themselves. Liturgy, a work of the people, needs to connect the paschal mystery with their needs and aspirations.

As a form of ritual activity, liturgy's effectiveness closely mirrors the moving force of any significant ritual. The following reflections are offered to enhance the liturgy.

*Bring the community a new transcendent level of experience and understanding through the liturgy.*

Meaningful rituals touch a deeper dimension that underpins life. In so doing they do not merely repeat a past event but bring it into the present. This can happen at a wedding anniversary celebration, birthday, a memorial, or religious ritual.

Effective rituals go beyond the functional and invite the participants into another dimension of space and time. They touch the sacred and connect the community more deeply with God. Whenever a ritual touches people's core, the repeatable aspects of ritual activity never leave the participants bored for they experience the realm of mystery. In connecting with the core level, liturgy touches this transcendent dimension. A prayerful atmosphere, moving music, reverent gestures, presider's style, and community faith help the congregation move beyond the immediate moment into this transcendent realm, where people experience the Lord in his paschal mystery.

*Make the liturgy the work of the people, not the vocation of a few professionals.*

If liturgical style becomes the exclusive domain of liturgical experts, it loses its heart and spirit, which dwell in the community itself. Excessive attention to liturgical exactness or going by the book leads to ossification of the rites. Here, more emphasis is placed on how to do the ritual than on how to respond to the living Lord dwelling in the faithful. To maintain its vigor, liturgy needs to develop along with the worshiping community. An ossified liturgical style is a real internal challenge in some Catholic parishes. Such a liturgy makes it difficult to maintain the flexibility needed for a welcoming atmosphere, amenable to today's generation of seekers.

To remain open to all people, parishes concern themselves with inculturation. This involves integrating liturgical actions with the cultural practices of various non-European ethnic groups, like Native Americans, African Americans, Puerto Ricans, Mexicans, Cubans, Chinese, Filipinos, Vietnamese, and Koreans. Effective parishes keep such diversity in mind and offer quality liturgies on Sundays and special occasions in accordance with the parish's ethnic makeup.

Inculturation has another face that transcends ethnic differences. Seldom do parishes consider ways to integrate liturgies with secular or technological culture. Such attention does not mean that liturgy assimilates superficial, functional elements. Rather, it acknowledges the shaping forces of secular culture, which affects a congregation's response to the liturgy. The spiritual vacuum created by secular society offers a rich opportunity to draw liturgical participants into a transcendent realm where silence, not noise, predominates, and where inspiring words, sacred music, and deep faith lead people to God.

### Avoid overemphasizing the rubrics.

Undue rigor in liturgy can suck the spirit out of liturgical celebrations. Vibrant liturgy needs two elements, namely, structure and spontaneity, which must be kept in balance. "Structure" without spontaneity leads to ossification of the ritual, while "spontaneity" without structure leads to confusion and chaos. Spontaneity must always happen within the boundaries established by approved liturgical directives. After Vatican II, spontaneity was overdone in many liturgies. Sometimes, this led to uncertainty about the celebration and to the disillusionment of the participants. Today, many liturgies are very structured. If overdone, this leads to a rigid formalism, which misses the transcendent dimension that overstructured liturgies may lack.

### Give emotional expression its proper place.

African American or Hispanic liturgies often energize the congregation. Such liturgical experiences contrast with the plastic, impersonal celebrations that other Catholics sometimes experience.

Parishes are invited to do more to engage the whole person, not merely the intellect, in liturgical worship. Effective liturgies enhance conversion, which involve the person's body, soul, and spirit.

## *Emphasize the Real Presence of Jesus in the Eucharist.*

Liturgical reforms of Vatican II established a balance among Christ's presence in the baptized community, the presider, the Word, and the Eucharist. Sometimes, the strong emphasis given to his presence in the Word and the believing community seemed to minimize his eucharistic presence. Jesus' Real Presence in the Eucharist is poorly understood by many Catholics. Some are ignorant of, or question, this central dogma of the Catholic faith. In an honor's theology course, a college student refused to accept Christ's Real Presence in the Eucharist because she did not believe his "physical fleshly body" was hidden somehow in the bread. Since this young woman had fourteen years of Catholic education, her misunderstanding of Christ's eucharistic presence surprised the professor. Upon further inquiry, he discovered that many other students had an equally poor understanding of the Church's teaching on the Real Presence. To refocus on it, liturgists and catechists can remember the words of *The Constitution on the Sacred Liturgy*, "At the Last Supper, on the night when he was betrayed, our Savior instituted the eucharistic sacrifice of His Body and Blood. He did this in order to perpetuate the sacrifice of the Cross throughout the centuries until he should come again..." (#47). Parish ministers need to focus on this fundamental Christian belief, teach it clearly, and give it priority.

Belief in Christ's eucharistic presence is at the core of the Church's life. A firm conviction about Jesus' Real Presence in the Eucharist makes it easier to recognize the connection between the Lord's living presence in our everyday lives and his paschal presence in the Eucharist. When the disillusioned disciples walked the road to Emmaus, they did not recognize Jesus until "…he had been made known to them in the breaking of the bread" (Luke 24:35). When troubled, we too can discover Jesus in the breaking of the bread.

Christian history discloses many devotions that honor Jesus' Real Presence in the Blessed Sacrament. Stressing Jesus' presence in the consecrated bread, these devotions continue their popularity with some Catholics. Today's eucharistic theology, while maintaining a firm belief in Christ's presence in the consecrated species, also stresses his eucharistic presence in the community and world. This is biblically, liturgically, and theologically based. When catechists and liturgists speak of Jesus' eucharistic presence, they need to emphasize his presence in the eucharistic species themselves and his presence in the action of Christians.

Liturgy is a powerful mode of evangelization. It celebrates what the Word proclaims and Christian service accomplishes. Imbued with a welcoming spirit, it mirrors Jesus' ministry. When this happens, our celebration of life and the liturgy become one act of praise to the God who made us.

## Give greater emphasis to the sacrament of reconciliation.

During Advent and Lent, many parishes offer a communal service of reconciliation with individual confessions. They also make available confessions on Saturdays before the evening liturgy. Few people avail themselves of this sacrament. It is not emphasized today and not much is done to foster its frequent reception. For many people the sacrament of reconciliation is the forgotten sacrament, and its been years since they have received it.

The infrequency of its use represents a significant change in Catholic sacramental life. Before Vatican II, this sacrament was celebrated regularly by most Catholics. Although the dwindling number of priests presents a challenge to its regular use, parish leaders need to look for creative ways to celebrate reconciliation on a more regular basis. It is an excellent way to stay tuned into one's spiritual journey and to obtain God's graces to face worldly temptations.

## Pastoral Suggestions

The following suggestions offer a parish specific ways to enhance liturgical celebrations:

- Have the liturgical or worship commission plan a seminar for adults, youth, and children, explaining the history and theology contained in the artwork in the parish church.

- Prepare a special welcome, including a brochure, for visitors and former Catholics who might come to the parish for Easter and Christmas Masses. Include in the brochure an invitation for inquirers and former Catholics to attend an "adult forum," focused on asking questions, venting frustrations, and seeking information.

- Set up an ad hoc committee to research and visit other parishes to ascertain creative ways to enhance the parish's devotional life.

- Invite a member of the diocesan worship or liturgical office or a liturgical minister from another parish to attend parish liturgies and liturgical commission meetings, look over parish liturgical plans, evaluate present liturgical practice, and offer suggestions to enhance the liturgy.

- Arrange for parish representatives to visit several Protestant churches to see how they welcome people, make them feel at home, and become involved in church affairs.

- Invite a speaker to address ways that parishioners can better prepare for and participate in Sunday liturgies.

- Invite a college professor or expert in theater to offer ways for the parish to better use drama and music in liturgical celebrations.

- At a worship commission meeting, reflect on the implications of seeing liturgical music as a form of evangelization.

- Twice yearly, arrange a late Sunday afternoon Mass, followed by a potluck dinner and discussion aimed at helping people who attend Mass every Sunday to better know one another.

- On one weekend in March, invite parishioners to give input on Sunday homilies and evaluate them through a flyer dropped in the collection basket.

- In late August, offer a seminar for parents, giving them practical suggestions to help them develop significant religious rituals in their homes.

- Offer an afternoon of reflection, sometime during the summer, on how to live and celebrate ordinary time.

- Have the pastoral associate or parish leaders visit a Protestant megachurch to study how it markets itself and its liturgies.

- Invite a Catholic college campus minister to offer a presentation to the parish council on how to attract seekers to Sunday liturgies and other liturgical functions.

- Once monthly, invite a representative from a different parish service to be in the church vestibule to provide information about this ministry.

- Have parish leaders evaluate the relationship between effective liturgical celebrations and the development of small faith communities in the parish.

- Provide money in the annual parish budget for members of the liturgical commission or interested parishioners to attend workshops to study ways to enhance the liturgy.

- Ask the liturgical commission to examine eucharistic adoration as a way to solidify Catholic identity, affirm Christ's Real Presence in the Eucharist, and enhance liturgical participation.

- During Advent and Lent, offer sessions on Sundays, between the Masses or at other times, on the history, theology, and current pastoral practice regarding the sacrament of reconciliation.

- Send a weekly e-mail to parishioners giving brief suggestions and meditations to help them prepare to celebrate the Sunday liturgy.

- In early fall, sponsor and invite an interested non-Catholic friend to an informal session for those interested in the RCIA.

- Have the liturgical commission discuss the wisdom of having a Catholic noneucharistic Sunday ritual of prayer and praise for seekers who do not attend Mass and who may choose such a mode of worship rather than attend Protestant worship services.

In *Excellent Catholic Parishes,* Paul Wilkes indicated that quality liturgy stood near the top in the excellent parishes that he surveyed. Vibrant liturgical celebrations are powerful ways to bring the Lord's presence into the hearts of believers and to inspire them to share Christ's eucharistic presence in their lives, families, and work. Faith-filled liturgy evangelizes and calls forth disciples to follow the Lord. This is the subject of Chapter Eight on christian service.

# 8.

# *Service Ministry*

My mother's hope chest remained unopened in the middle room of our family home for over twenty years. One day, she asked me to examine its contents with her. We went through the memorabilia that she had gathered over the years. Her sewing materials and remnants of cloth, carefully packed on one side, were saved from our family's small dry goods store. A pack of cards, carefully arranged, was lying in the corner. It contained an envelope addressed to Mom at Good Samaritan Hospital, Cincinnati, Ohio, dated February 8, 1934. Seeing it, I felt something stir deep inside me. The card contained a note from Dad to Mom sent right after I was born on February 2, 1934. He told her to hurry home. The card also disclosed his sense of humor, for within it was a still-intact piece of chewing gum with the note, "If you need it, here is something to hold the baby's diaper." We found all sorts of other memorabilia in the hope chest, including Mom's high school graduation picture, one of Dad as a child, and pictures of me, my brother, and my sisters. I found my old baseball and many more wonderful treasures.

When almost finished examining the contents, I noticed a piece of brown material with a hole cut out about the size of a person's head. Upon seeing it, I realized that it was no ordinary scrap of cloth. Shortly after beginning the first grade, I became very sick and had to stay home for almost the entire year. Mom taught me there. Each day, she walked across the street to St. William's school to get my lessons.

As that Christmas approached, the first grade was planning for a pageant in church. Sister Mary Paul, the teacher, invited me to be a shepherd. Mom made me a shepherd's outfit from the old piece of cloth that I now held in my hands. When pageant day came, Sister Mary Paul helped me put on my shepherd's head covering fastening it on my head with a pin. When I told her that I felt "a hurt in my head," she replied, "Bob, don't worry, for it may be a bit too tight, but it will loosen up."

During the pageant my head throbbed. After the service I had a splitting headache. When we returned to the church undercroft, I tried to take off the headpiece. It would not release, so I called Sister Mary Paul. Seeing what had happened, she said, "Bob, I am so sorry. I accidentally pinned the covering through the skin of your head."

Over the years, I often joked with Mom about the fine outfit she had made for me and how it was pinned into my head. What a joy to see the old piece of cloth out of which she had fashioned the headpiece over sixty years ago. What a greater joy to have her sitting right next to me as we recounted the old story!

As we closed the hope chest, I reflected on Christian service. On that pleasant April day, when Mom and I looked through the old memorabilia, it became clearer that Christian service begins in the home. The greatest service ever provided me was the gift of my parents' time and talents. This included innumerable hours that Mom sat next to me, as we did that day, teaching me my lessons, while Dad worked in our store to support the family. It extended to Mom's cooking and sewing and Dad's showing us how to play ball. As we grew older, it flowered in my work in our family business. I learned more about serving others from my father's example in the store than I ever learned from books. My parents' dedication set firm patterns of responsibility for their children. This foundation rooted the deep value of our service to family, Church, society, and world.

Jesus' call to service is at the heart of Christian evangelization, which I first witnessed in family life. The parish supplements what happens in the family. This chapter considers the parish and the ministry of service in three parts, namely, Parish Ministry and Jesus' Call to Serve, Social Ministry in the Family and Society, and Pastoral Suggestions.

## Parish Ministry and Jesus' Call to Serve

My parents taught me Jesus' call to serve through their very lives. Without their example, I would not have heard Jesus' call in the same way. Perhaps I never may have heard it at all. Contemporary children and teenagers need to see examples of service. Some people hear this call through parental example or the inspiration of loved ones, others sense it through various life experiences. At its deepest level the call to serve comes from God's living Spirit, inspiring us in the core of our being. Parents, teachers, and parish ministers help people, especially the young, to identify God as the spiritual source of their desire to serve.

Many young adults work with Habitat for Humanity or inner-city soup kitchens. Others spend vacations or time after graduation volunteering in third-world countries or the United States. The Catholic Church with a rich history of social justice affords many opportunities to serve under the auspices of its various organizations. Such knowledge can help people see how the Church lifts up those caught in poverty. *In All Things Charity (IATC),* the U.S. bishops say,

"The history of the Church reveals a long tradition of defending those living in poverty, supporting charitable institutions, and promoting justice" (p. 8).

Biblical tradition roots the Church's commitment to the poor. This begins in the Old Testament and is articulated in the Sinai covenant made between God and the Jewish nation. God promised fidelity to the Hebrew nation, and the Jews promised to follow the commandments that God gave them, "made explicit in the great legal codes. Integral to those codes is the special concern charged to the community for the widows, orphans, and strangers who comprised God's beloved poor" (*IATC*, p. 12).

Jesus centered his teaching on the great commandment to love God and our neighbor, and especially to minister to the poor. His quotation from the prophet Isaiah that he had been sent "to bring good news to the poor"—reminds us of our responsibility to reach out to the least of our bothers and sisters (Luke 4:18–19). *In All Things Charity* states, "In his ministry, Jesus healed the sick and disabled, returning them to good health and to their families and communities. He thus embodied the compassion of God and set relationships right within the community....[He affirmed and proclaimed] an essential equality of dignity among all human beings, men and women, whatever their ethnic origin, nation, or race, culture, political membership or social condition" (p. 14, referring to *Guidelines for the Study and Teaching of the Church's Social Doctrine in the Formation of Priests*, §16).

Jesus' ministry to the poor establishes the foundation for the parish's call to service. The first Christian communities distributed their goods to the poor, ministered to orphans and widows, and chose deacons to serve the needy (*IATC*, p. 15). Parishes are invited to do the same. As living symbols of justice and charity, they are safe harbors where the poor, sick, and hurt find solace and help. The U.S. Catholic Bishops emphasized the need for parishes to stress the Church's social tradition, by stating, "We urge pastors, staff, and volunteers to be sensitive to the social mission of the Church in prayer and worship, preaching and education, support for parishioners' daily lives and work, outreach and charity, legislative action and community organizing, and global solidarity" (*IATC*, p. 23).

Serving the poor is the special responsibility of the pastor, who sets the tone for this ministry by nature of his priestly ordination. As Pope John Paul II says, the ordained ministry "is completely at the service of the Church" (*Pastores dabo vobis*, §16). In addition, the *Instruction on Certain Questions Regarding the Collaboration of the Non-Ordained Faithful in the Sacred Ministry of Priests* says, "Intrinsically linked to the sacramental nature of ecclesial ministry is its character of service..." ("Theological Principles," par. 8). The ordained minister is the symbol that Jesus' service ministry is happening throughout the parish—in families, neighborhoods, workplaces, and wherever parishioners are.

The priest witnesses to Jesus' call, inviting Christians to reach out to the needy, when he presides at the eucharistic liturgy. *In All Things Charity* describes the central role of the eucharistic celebration in furthering the Church's social mission when it says, "The greatest gift that we have received from the Lord Jesus is the Eucharist....As the parish gathers for the celebration of the Eucharist, the needs and rights of the poor and disenfranchised must be placed on the table....The Word proclaimed in the Eucharist must affirm and celebrate the parish's work for charity, justice, and peace. The Word must inspire social analysis and concerted action, leading the people of God to a renewed commitment to the poor" (pp. 23–24).

The parish community, gathered for the Eucharist, remembers that "as Catholics we are called to take concrete measures to overcome the misunderstandings, ignorance, competition, and fear that stand in the way of genuinely welcoming the stranger in our midst and enjoying the communion that is our destiny as Children of God" (*Unity in Diversity,* p. 31).

As the symbol of unity among Catholics, the Eucharist challenges parishes to reach out to immigrants. *Unity in Diversity* says, "Immigrants will experience the Church's welcome most personally at the level of the parish. Pastors and parish staff, accordingly, must be filled with a spirit of welcome, responding to a new and perhaps little-understood culture" (p. 43). As immigrants increasingly enter our neighborhoods, showing them the love of Christ and inviting them to share their gifts with the community are powerful ways to evangelize them.

## Social Ministry in the Family and Society

Parish ministers assist the congregation in prayer, praise of God, and service to one another. Their leadership deepens the parish's prayer life and helps parishioners reach out to their families and society. Parish ministers are to make serious efforts to create an "attitude of service" throughout the parish. Such an attitude gives high priority to helping parishioners accept responsibility to serve in their families, workplace, and neighborhood. When this attitude permeates all parish functions, programs, ministries, and organizations, it affects pastoral council decisions, finance commission matters, liturgical celebrations, preaching, catechesis, and the organizations serving the poor.

Parish ministers take the lead in overall parish service activities by developing systems that help needy people within and beyond the parish. Many parishes already have organizations to help the poor, like the St. Vincent de Paul Society or the Ladies of Charity. Other parishes encourage parishioners to assist in hospitals and retirement centers. Still others help immigrants to find jobs or learn English. How parishes fulfill the demands of the gospel varies from region to region.

## Focus on the Family

In addition to organized parish efforts, effective pastoral ministers focus on the family. In *A Family Perspective in Church and Society*, the U.S. bishops emphasize this family attitude, saying, "As a systems orientation, a family perspective is a lens that focuses on the interaction between individuals, their families, and social situations" (p. 8). This means that whatever a parish does, it takes the family into account when planning parish programs and events.

Parishes today acknowledge the existence of many different family configurations. These include nuclear, divorced, blended, and single-parent families, and children living with relatives. Regardless of the family composition, parishes focus on inviting them to become domestic churches or churches of the home.

Parish ministers remind family members that a lifelong orientation toward service begins in the home. Christian service, learned from early childhood, blooms as children mature. It calls a person beyond one's immediate family to see oneself as a minister of the Lord, called to serve the larger society. High school, college, and older persons may not realize that their gifts in mathematics, computer science, nursing, teaching, construction, or administration are given to them by God to serve their neighbor. Such a realization gives an individual a new sense of purpose. In a world where millions of people starve and the gap widens between rich and poor, parishes that preach Jesus' message of justice take a forward step in overcoming social inequalities.

Parishes can encourage parishioners to serve the poor in two ways. First, some people may directly serve hungry, hurting, and broken people through personal efforts or charity. Catholic social agencies, religious communities, parishes, and individuals respond to people's immediate needs by direct service to the poor. Second, others may work to change the social structures that keep people oppressed. Christian employees, managers, and executives are challenged to root out systemic injustices in both the private and public sectors. This responsibility includes working to eliminate unjust social structures that keep people in poverty and boycotting products manufactured in third-world sweatshops owned by United States corporations where workers receive substandard wages for products sold at huge profits in this country.

Catholic business and social leaders are challenged to reject unjust corporate policies, even though doing so may threaten their job security or economic future in institutions that exist for the "bottom line." Society needs prophetic voices in corporate boardrooms and business meetings where just decisions could change those systems that keep people in poverty. Catholics on the top rung of the economic ladder can make inroads into unjust systems if they are brave enough to hear Jesus' message and bold enough to do something about it.

## Shepherding in Society and World

Often the roots of personal commitment to serve spring from the example learned in our families. For example, my own home environment fostered an invitation to service, symbolized in the large crucifix and the statue of the Good Shepherd that Mom placed in our living room years ago.

We gain insights into Christian service through this biblical image of Jesus as the Good Shepherd. The historical image of the shepherd has two faces. The first pictures a respected person, symbolized by King David, a shepherd. The second shows a broken and poor shepherd, an image common at Jesus' time. When Jesus called himself the Good Shepherd, both images come to mind. In Jesus, the king of kings and the royal shepherd assumes the stance of the lowly shepherd to teach us an important lesson about Christian service.

Who are the good shepherds today? In answering this question, it helps to remember the two images of the shepherd. Each serves its function in various stages of our lives. The positive image applies at those times when we have power, respect, and importance. The negative image is relevant when we are weak, broken, and hurt.

Sometimes we are important, admired, and in control. This is the situation of all parents with small children who are powerless before adults. It also applies when an individual has a responsible position in business or civic affairs. Such times provide special opportunities to shepherd or serve.

Parental influence is incalculable in a child's physical, psychological, and spiritual development. The Good Shepherd statue in our home symbolized how our parents served us and prepared us for a life of Christian service. This type of unarticulated service is the highest form of evangelization.

Executives, managers, nurses, doctors, and teachers have many chances to shepherd their associates or employees by showing them opportunities and pitfalls in the office, school, marketplace, or on a business trip. "Marketplace service" is an important way to share Christ's call to make disciples of all nations.

There are also times when we are powerless. We may be broken by sickness, devastated by a loved one's death, or worried about a job loss. Such occasions can lead us to withdraw, feel sorry for ourselves, or despair. Rarely do we view these occasions as opportunities to serve as a good shepherd by accepting our brokenness as Jesus did, and by ministering out of weakness, not strength. At such times, the image of Jesus as the Good Shepherd is a powerful invitation to find our strength in God so that we may serve humankind.

The following story tells of Sally, a modern shepherd, ministering in a real-life situation. She was a single, hardworking, Catholic woman. When she moved into her home twenty years ago, Sam and Nora, an older couple with no children or living relatives, lived next door. They were self-sufficient and independent, having little to do with Sally except for a casual "hello."

This pattern continued for ten years until Sam became sick and died. Alone now, Nora rarely came out of her home. Sally began to visit and console her. As time passed and Nora's health declined, Sally spent more time with her.

Religion or God was never mentioned during these visits, for Nora wanted it this way. One evening, when leaving Nora's home, Sally said, "God bless you!" Nora's countenance sparkled. This simple blessing initiated a remarkable change in her.

As Nora's physical and spiritual needs increased, Sally visited her several times daily. At the end of each day Sally sat on the arm of Nora's large chair. They prayed the Our Father and Hail Mary. One day Sally said, "Nora, do you remember that nice priest who visited you in the hospital? Would you want him to come and see you at home?" Nora agreed. For several months Father Paul visited her regularly. He often began by saying, "Nora, I've had a hard day. Do you mind if I sit with you in your living room? It helps me relax." Soon they began talking about God and the Catholic church. As Nora neared death, Father Paul anointed her and gave her communion. In her last hours Nora asked Sally, "When will God call me home?" She replied, "It will be soon. Then you will see Jesus waiting for you with his arms open. The Good Shepherd will rejoin you with Sam, your husband, and you will live in joy forever."

After Nora's burial Sally said, "Through my entire experience with Nora, it was not really me who was acting. It was the Spirit of the Living Christ acting through me. Because of God's Spirit, Nora changed and I changed. Never again will I be the same."

Sally was a good shepherd because she allowed the Spirit of the Risen Christ to live through her. There is no greater witness, no greater evangelization, than the testimony of one's life given for a needy brother or sister. The image of the Good Shepherd shows us that the entire Body of Christ is responsible for Christian service.

Because of Sally and Nora's story, I now see more clearly what is symbolized by the beautiful, original paint on face and hands of the Good Shepherd statue sitting in my mother's living room. Its color is as bright and shiny as the day it was painted over one hundred years ago, because the face and hands are those of Christ. In contrast, the remaining paint on Christ's clothes have flaked off. Now I see this broken, chipped paint as symbolizing us—the broken Body of Christ. Whenever we shepherd others out of weakness, the power represented by Christ's hands and feet overcomes our brokenness and we become Christ in our time.

In reflecting on the Good Shepherd, we are reminded that the U.S. Catholic Church has many committed permanent deacons who symbolize through their service that all Christians are called to serve. They are living witnesses of the commitment the Church has made since apostolic days to reach out to the needy and poor.

The 1971 Synod document *Justice in the World* states, "Action on the behalf of justice and participation in the transformation of the world fully appear to us as a constitutive dimension of the preaching of the Gospel, or, in other words, of the church's mission for the redemption of the human race and its liberation from every oppressive situation" (Introduction). These words invite parishes to renew their ministry to the poor.

In saying that justice ministry is a "constitutive dimension of the Gospel," the Synod implies that proclaiming the gospel in word or action is incomplete without justice ministry. Christian service is not a voluntary activity but an essential demand of the Gospel. Therefore, no parish fulfills its responsibility unless it proclaims and lives justice through its ministries. To do so, a parish is to include the justice dimension its mission and to live it through the ministries of Word, worship, and service. In particular, a parish peace and justice commission has a special responsibility to keep the parish focused on the gospel's social demands.

## Pastoral Suggestions

Living the call to justice is important because our society emphasizes individualism and greed. Justice ministry requires an overall orientation that pervades the entire parish. The following suggestions are intended to help parishes keep the gospel's justice demand in the forefront.

- Ask the pastoral council to incorporate a justice perspective into a parish's mission statement.
- At a staff day of renewal, evaluate the parish's general orientation and specific ministries, looking at how seriously the parish commits itself to Jesus' call to justice.
- Remind parishioners often through bulletin announcements, homilies, liturgical celebrations, and catechesis that every Christian is called to act justly in one's individual life, family, and work.
- Articulate clearly in parish policies and activities the significance of the family as setting the foundations for Christian service.
- Monitor and evaluate parish service organizations to ensure that the needs of parishioners and neighbors are met.
- Appoint an ad hoc committee to study the issue of twinning (a collaborative effort) with a needy parish in the diocese or other location to further the cause of the gospel.
- Remind parishioners in Sunday homilies and bulletin announcements of their vocation to bring Christian social values into their family, marketplace, and neighborhood.
- Invite the parish justice commission to set up a process to develop new service ministries to address the needs of immigrants.

- Work with agencies, such as the United Way, that have a proven, systematic way of helping the poor, to address the social and economic needs of parishioners and neighbors.

- Ask the parish ecumenical commission to develop a plan for cooperating with Christian, Jewish, Muslim, Buddhist, and other religions in the area to assist the needy.

- Through Sunday bulletin announcements, collect used cell phones for the poor and distribute them to people needing them for security in unsafe areas.

- Invite an interested parish group to offer an occasional seminar for people who have to deal with alcohol or drug problems.

- Have an accountant in the parish conduct a workshop on estate planning and keeping financial records for the elderly or other interested parishioners.

- In the parish bulletin or on the Web site, list parishioners who celebrate their birthdays that week.

- Ask the men's society or a parish prayer group to arrange for a monthly early-morning parish breakfast centered around "Faith and Work."

- Announce monthly in the bulletin or on the web site various volunteer service opportunities available in hospitals, soup kitchens, or other places in the area.

- Ask the social-justice commission to prioritize the justice needs within the parish and neighborhood.

- Arrange to have a parishioner teach citizenship or foreign language classes for ethnic groups in the parish, or find places where such classes are available and advertise them in the bulletin and on the Web site.

- Request that the social-justice commission or youth ministry director study various possibilities for outreach and ministry to people in missionary areas.

- Have the coordinator of ministry to the homebound and hospitalized keep an updated record of the sick in the parish, so that cards, prayers, and greetings can be sent to them.

- Work with other Christian churches in the area to help support a food bank and homeless center.

- Contact the Paulist Evangelization Center or some other such group to see what possibilities exist to conduct a parish evangelization mission centered around family and work.

- Have the parish youth ministry director arrange an afternoon of reflection for teens on ways that young people can perform service ministry.

- Offer a Sunday afternoon of reflection for young adults centering on how evangelizing and ministering in one's job is part of one's calling by God.

- Have the pastoral council look into the need for a paid or volunteer counselor to directly assist parishioners with personal issues or to help them connect with a good private counselor or public service agency.

- Invite the pastor and pastoral council to investigate ways to create an overall attitude of service in the parish so that it becomes known as a "caring community."

- Invite a member of the parish staff to look into the growing movement of "parish nurses" who serve the community in healing ministry and investigate the need of such a ministry in the parish.

As parishes change, new social and spiritual needs emerge. These open the door for fresh approaches to evangelization and ministry. While reflecting on the relationship between evangelization and service, Paul VI's words are worth remembering, "Evangelization is in fact the grace and vocation proper to the Church, her deepest identity. She exists in order to evangelize" (*Evangelii Nuntiandi*, §14).

The parish follows in the spirit of Christ when it reaches out to the poor. *The Gospel of Life* says, "Evangelization is an all-embracing, progressive activity through which the Church participates in the prophetic, priestly, and royal mission of the Lord Jesus. It is, therefore, inextricably linked to *preaching, celebration and the service of charity.* Evangelization is a *profoundly ecclesial act,* which calls all the various workers of the Gospel to action, according to their individual charisms and ministry" (§78).

Service is at the heart of the gospel, which evangelization proclaims. Parishes motivated by the Spirit take seriously their call to serve. Implementing this call to serve is addressed in Part Four, "Realizing the Vision."

PART FOUR

*Realizing the Vision—*
*The World and the Parish:*
*Present and Future*

# 9.

# *Challenging a Parish's Vision*

Father Jack was appointed to St. Edward's Parish after the death of its former pastor. Father Jack listened to parishioners and made no changes for the first year. Everything went well and the people soon came to love this saintly man. During his second year, the parishioners asked him to strengthen youth catechesis. With the support of the pastoral council, he hired a catechetical leader. She formed a committee made up of Father Jack, parents, and catechists. They selected textbooks, prepared catechists, and advertised the new program.

The week after the new program was launched, Father Jack invited Emily, the diocesan catechetical director, to dinner at the parish with the committee. After dinner they began to discuss their progress in revitalizing youth catechesis. But the discussion soon turned somber. Father Jack said, "Emily, we launched our program last Wednesday. Our catechetical director did a great job of recruiting catechists, getting new textbooks, and contacting students through written invitations. The catechists went to seminars and prepared themselves. Something went wrong, however, and we are unsure how to fix it." Emily responded, "Sounds like you did everything right. What happened?" The catechetical director replied, with embarrassment "On the first night, the catechists waited in their rooms but no students showed up. We don't know what to do."

Emily was puzzled. When she arrived for dinner, young people were milling around the playground and inside the gym. She said, "I need some clarification. There are plenty of teenagers outside right now." Father Jack replied, "Tonight is Tuesday; it's youth gym and recreation night. The high school students from this parish go to six different schools in various parts of the city. They look forward to coming on Tuesday evening to have fun with their friends. The coordinator of youth activities does a great job in getting them here. We don't have the same success with our catechetical program." Emily said, "Have you ever tired to coordinate both programs since the young people will not come here two nights a week? Why not invite the youth coordinator and several teenagers to join your committee? Hopefully, you can solve the problem together. I'd recommend joining the two programs into one unified parish youth ministry by making catechesis a regular part of the Tuesday event." The parish did this and the program succeeded.

This story illustrates that well-meaning pastoral ministers who develop excellent programs may still not succeed in getting people to come unless they take into account the social and cultural context of those involved. The young people in this parish were not lazy. They could not afford the time to come to the parish twice weekly. Forced to choose between the two programs, they gave a higher priority to socializing with friends than to receiving catechesis.

This chapter addresses the vital role that a cultural context plays in successful parish ministry. The first eight chapters of this book focused on Jesus' core message and the community's role in celebrating this message. Throughout these chapters, stories and illustrations stressed the importance of acknowledging parishioner's needs. The final three chapters look primarily at how to connect Jesus' message with people's needs. In so doing, it is vitally important to be sensitive to the cultural context of those involved. St. Edward's Parish ministers missed this in preparing their catechetical program. In any place where ministry happens, culture is key to ministerial success.

Since a parish's vision takes shape in a given culture, the parish is ever changing, not a historical monument. Parish effectiveness depends on how well it responds to the needs of parishioners living in a highly secular culture. The *Constitution on the Church in the Modern World* challenges parishes to rub shoulders with the world and transform it in light of the gospel. In accepting this challenge, parishes need to address economic, social, and political issues, including racism, economic injustice, arms control, nuclear warfare, and right-to-life questions. This is the only effective way to evangelize modern society.

Social responsibility—which increases in a highly efficient, functional, materialistic, and pragmatic world— invites parishes to become actively involved in society's problems but not to succumb to its secularizing influences. For a parish to deal effectively with the challenges it faces, clear directions are necessary. Its response must center on God's love, disclosed through the lived presence of the Spirit in the Catholic community.

Knowing the challenges does little to shift a parish's focus unless it does something about them. Society exercises a pervasive influence on parish ministries. When a parish addresses this influence in light of the gospel, it evangelizes society. Acknowledging the interface between society and gospel is foundational for developing a viable parish vision.

This chapter looks at Society's Basic Orientation, Aspects of American Society, and Pastoral Suggestions.

## Society's Basic Orientation

Catholic theology sees the world as good, but wounded by sin. It is good because God made it and continues to dwell here. This positive attitude is the basis for our pastoral approach to ministry in secular society. We see the world through the lens of faith. We acknowledge that all nature reflects God's grandeur; we recognize divine footprints in the woods, meadows, oceans, rivers, plants, and animals that populate our earthly garden. We also find God's presence in the marvels of technology, including medicine, television, and computers. Finally, we affirm that God loves us because we are made in the divine image.

The Catholic theology of creation teaches that after the Fall of Adam and Eve, God did not abandon humankind. We are not corrupt, but wounded. This makes us prone to sin, suffering, and death. After the Fall, we are still made in God's image through the indwelling of the Spirit who graces us because of our relationship with God.

Catholic theology emphasizes our basic goodness, while admitting our imperfections. It recognizes how medicine, agriculture, technology, and science have produced a better world. Microphones, electric wheelchairs, automobiles, and computers add to God's glory and our benefit. It sees God's finger in both the humanities and the achievements of modern science and technology, which we can use for God's greater glory and humankind's benefit.

As graced creatures, we continue God's work on earth. Jesus calls us to reach out to the poor, widowed, handicapped, and aged. Pope John Paul II calls this type of witness "everyday heroism," saying it is "made up of gestures of sharing, big or small, which build up an authentic culture of life" (*Gospel of Life,* §86). Such heroism happens in our families, neighborhoods, schools, and workplaces.

Catholic belief in God's grace, nature's basic goodness, and human responsibility underpin the faith perspective from which we view humanitarian and scientific developments that have occurred since the beginning of history. These have intensified during the past hundred years as science and technology took great strides forward. In this regard, *Gaudium et Spes*, speaking of the faithful, says, "Let them blend new sciences and theories and the understanding of the most recent discoveries with Christian morality and the teaching of Christian doctrine, so that their religious culture and morality may keep pace with scientific knowledge and with the constantly progressing technology" (§62).

## Aspects of American Society

Our society challenges Catholics to live their faith and avoid the temptation to serve the world rather than God and neighbor. *Gaudium et Spes* says, "...the Church has always had the duty of scrutinizing the signs of the times and of interpreting them in the light of the Gospel" (§4).

### Materialism

Society emphasizes worldly matters. Rock music, television, and advertising tell us that happiness is found in pleasure, power, and money. People buy status automobiles, bigger homes, violent toys, and designer clothes. The world's allurements engulf this generation, and the attraction makes it difficult for us to realize that material possessions are not the answer. A similar dynamic that moved the rich young man of the Gospel to walk away from Jesus challenges us.

Søren Kierkegaard, a nineteenth-century Danish Lutheran philosopher, said that times such as ours are like people who woke up one day and found themselves dead. Sensing the effects of secularism, he predicted the hollowness of future generations. The vacuum that many people experience in their lives leads them on a journey to discover their spiritual core. This is manifested in the current hunger for prayer, scripture studies, spiritual friendship, altruism, ecological awareness, and the quest for justice. These intensify at the same time as people recognize the limits of materialism.

### Money

Even though people recognize the limits of materialism, money is still central in our society, even on a parish level. Its pervasive influence sometimes is clouded by the implicit assumption that parish effectiveness is driven by its financial resources. While money is necessary in our society and parishes need it to finance their ministries, the best-financed ministries will fail if they are not rooted in the teachings of Jesus. While keeping monetary priorities in balance, parishes also have to recognize the tensions present when finances are lacking. This causes friction among competing interests. Money is one but not the major factor in deciding how the Catholic faith is lived and celebrated in a parish.

A parish needs to consider the broader stewardship question, which includes a parishioner's time, talents, and treasure. Stewardship calls a parish to an awareness of its social responsibilities, which are linked with evangelization. This is community centered and transcends monetary concerns. Pope John Paul II challenges us not to become overly involved in materialistic society but to concentrate on the gospel. He says, "Against the spirit of the world, the Church takes up anew each day a struggle that is none other than *the struggle for the world's soul*" (*Crossing the Threshold of Hope*, p. 112).

## Cultural Relativism and Individualism

This "struggle for the world's soul" is reflected in the pervasive influence of cultural relativism, which rejects absolute norms of right and wrong. These are independent of how people personally think, feel, or believe. Affirming the existence of moral absolutes, particularly with young people, brings disagreement from those who argue that right or wrong depends on each person's conscience. This leads to the conclusion that one person's belief is as good as another.

Centering belief in the individual, relativism teaches that no objective norms of right and wrong exist. It challenges core Christianity, for the Judeo-Christian tradition teaches that morality has an objective reference point in God's law that is independent of personal opinions or subjective beliefs.

Effective parish ministry stresses absolute norms of right and wrong and points out the contradictions inherent in a lifestyle that affirms that everything is relative. Put in another way, "Conversion to Jesus Christ implies walking in his footsteps" (*GDC*, #85).

## Individualism and Individuality

Individualism, which relativism affirms, is different from individuality. The latter, a God-given gift, makes us who we are in a community of persons. In recognizing our individuality we accept the responsibilities that accompany it.

Knowing our personal gifts helps us grow in wisdom, holiness, and service to our brothers and sisters.

Individualism, a distortion of individuality, minimizes the common good and breeds selfishness and lack of concern for others. The degree of individuality in American society can manifest itself through the lens of another culture. Dr. Marcia worked in an employment agency for thirty years. During this time she asked people from other cultures what in United States culture was different from theirs. Almost all replied, "The major difference is your families. Our families are more closely knit and do things together as a family. We seem to eat with and enjoy one another more than you do. Your society's individualism affects your families. The results are not good."

Ours is a "me culture," where being #1 is a high priority. This breeds selfishness, reflected in statements like, "I don't go to Mass because I don't get anything out of it" or "I skipped Sunday Mass because I wanted to watch a football game." Creating a parish community atmosphere is difficult because of people's personal agendas and the distractions in their lives.

## Leisure, Pressures, and Preoccupations

We have many opportunities for rest, excitement, and leisure, including sports, concerts, plays, nature walks, and other outdoor activities. Often, we do not take advantage of them. Coupled with easy access to television, theater, games, and the Internet, time passes quickly. So much to do and so many opportunities to do it make it difficult to balance the time given to work, family, worship, and service.

Parents struggle with job demands and feel guilty when they do not spend more time with their family. Some overcompensate, lavishing their children with expensive gifts at Christmas or on birthdays. Undue lavishness spoils children and thrusts them into the same secular vortex that challenges their parents. This easily leads to dysfunctional behavior when their emotional needs are unfulfilled.

Parents spend considerable energy on children's activities, especially sports. Sometimes this challenges parishes. Near a large Catholic parish, a neighborhood playground has ten soccer fields. Each Sunday morning, Catholic children at various stages of soccer development fill these fields. They play soccer games at the same time that the parish celebrates Mass. Many of these Catholic children do not go to church on Sunday. Neither do their parents, who accompany them to their games instead of taking them to church. Such parental actions send a powerful message to children that soccer is more important than Mass.

## Technology and Mobility

As technology becomes more pervasive, "...the Church must appropriate all the positive values of culture and reject those elements which impede development of the true potential of persons and people" (*GDC*, #21). Parishes affirm culture's positive values by stressing the advances made in technology, communications, food production, medicine, and science. They encourage parishioners to see their work as an opportunity to further the mission of Christ, for Catholics believe that the living God dwells in this world and can be seen in a person's face, nature's beauty, and human work.

People hunger for the positive moral values that good television programs can bring into our homes. Unfortunately, many programs stress violence, sex, and greed. They blunt spiritual values and reinforce a materialistic, amoral world-view. Coupled with certain Internet material, these values run counter to what Jesus instructed his disciples to proclaim.

Rather than make it easier for working people, technology has increased the demands on them. Time is in short supply, people find it hard to balance family life and work pressures, and job security is lacking. With downsizing, corporate takeovers, and bottom-line economics, few workers have stability in their lives.

Catholic social teaching challenges industrialized nations to focus on the rights of persons, for the basis for "all human rights rest in the dignity of the person" (*Church in America*, §57). Pope John Paul II also says, "The Church in America is called…to cooperate with every legitimate means in reducing the negative effects of globalization…especially in the economic sphere, and the loss of the values of local cultures in favor of a misguided homogenization" (§55).

People struggle to balance job pressures and other responsibilities. This causes tension, reflected in the words of a high school student who said, "My family has moved five times in the past seven years. These frequent moves discourage us from developing new friendships or getting active in the parish." His father agreed, saying, "After moving often it's too painful to get close to neighbors or make new friends and then be uprooted from them." Asking why he continued his present career path, he replied, "With five children, we must move to support our family."

It's not easy to minister to a highly mobile parish population. In one suburban mid-western parish, one third of the parishioners move each year. Such mobility challenge parishes to develop effective ministerial plans.

## Stability, Roots, and Morality

Besides a place to call home, people search for a consistent creed of conduct. They instinctively realize that if absolutes are absent, relativism rules, and moral values disappear or become muted. What happens on the small scale happens on the larger scale. Take the example of lying. Many people think little about lying if they get away with it. Such attitudes affect corporate America, politics, families, and children. When a basic foundation of society, like telling the truth, is maintained, society thrives. When it disappears, society collapses.

A consistent way of life is at the core of Jesus' teaching. John Paul II says, "The Gospel of life is at the heart of Jesus' message. Lovingly received day after day by the Church, it is to be preached with dauntless fidelity as 'good news' to the people of every age and culture" (*Gospel of Life, §1*) These words challenge the leveling of moral values, which shreds the seamless robe of human life.

When families and educational environments teach solid moral values, children develop a positive regard for others. Most Americans respect their neighbors, but an increasing number resort to violence to solve their problems. Though society respects children's rights, abortion kills millions of innocent children. And even as we provide better care for elderly citizens, pressure groups encourage euthanasia and assisted suicide. Such inconsistencies, resulting from the lack of a consistent life ethic, challenge parishes to speak out for life and to minister to people struggling with such issues.

## Fear and Anger

People fear being cheated in business, over the phone, or in home solicitation. Many hesitate to walk down the street or to send their children to school. Divorce, job loss, uncertain futures, and personal rejection leave some adults angry. This influences their children and sometimes leads to school violence.

Jesus taught us to overcome fear with faith, violence with forgiveness, and greed with generosity. As John Paul II says, "Every sign of servile fear vanishes before the awesome power of the all-powerful and all-present One. Its place is taken by filial concern, in order that God's will be done on earth—that will which is the good that has in Him its origin and its ultimate fulfillment" *(Crossing the Threshold of Hope,* pp. 226–27).

## A Road Map and Credible Authority

Jesus offers searching people a roadmap, a trustworthy role model, and a reason why they are on earth. The *Baltimore Catechism* says that we are created to know, love, and serve God, so that we might be happy with him forever in heaven (#3 & 4). People look for this kind of clear message, which is more instructive than the secular gospel. Many children, lacking a road map of what is right and wrong, turn to television, the Internet, and music for their answers. Unable to sort out positive values for themselves, children often put unrealistic demands on parents and teachers. When parents lack the courage to say "no" and face the resulting tantrums, their children often grow up devoid of discipline.

People seek credible authority in family, politics, business, and church. Few Americans trust leaders just because they are in charge. This climate offers parish ministers an opportunity to become servant leaders, whom people accept.

People respect authority not because an individual holds a position but because he or she is a trustworthy servant.

## Bigness and Bureaucracy

Many people associate being successful with bigness. An RCIA candidate recounted that bigness is the greatest challenge that society presents her. She said, "Everything is big—homes, bureaucracy, Internet, and churches. How can we live intimate, community-based lives amidst such bigness? For me, small communities within a parish are one answer."

Size is not a good monitor of success. A person may receive better medical treatment from a country doctor than a high-profile city physician, even though advanced medical procedures may require a specialist in a large hospital facility. The goal of a business career is not always to become a corporate president. Many individuals find their niche in a self-employed position rather than in a corporate structure. Some Catholics prefer smaller parishes, which may minister more effectively than large ones. Large parishes need to ask, "How do we create a community environment within the parish itself? To accomplish this goal one pastor divided the parish into 150 neighborhood units, each with a captain who saw to it that people in his or her unit felt connected with the larger parish.

## Balance

Balancing the multiple demands of society is not easy. Even though many people come to grips with family, work, and social responsibilities, their efforts leave them stressed. To make sense of their lives, some turn to religion, join parishes, search out Christian groups, engage in Bible study, or volunteer in ministry.

Tired and irritable people can neglect their faith, children, spouses, parents, and neighbors. They often find it easier to eat in fast-food restaurants than prepare meals at home. Children, stressed at home, carry this into their classrooms where their acting out often is a cry for help.

The first step to assist parishioners with such life pressures is to avoid putting more pressure on them by asking too much of them for parish ministries. Parish staffs need to consider how much they ask volunteers to absent themselves from their families for parish ministry.

## Pastoral Suggestions

Our society establishes the climate within which a parish develops its ministries. To assist in this process, the following pastoral suggestions are offered:

- Ask the social-action commission to invite a sociologist to address the ministerial staff and volunteer ministers on how society impacts parish attendance and ministry.

- Before developing or revising a parish mission statement or ministerial plan, have parish leaders and staff members participate in a seminar on social and ethnic perspectives that affect the parish.

- Invite the pastoral ministry coordinator to arrange an afternoon of reflection for parish council and staff members, centering on the spiritual needs of children, youth, adults, and seniors.

- During Lent, plan sessions for parish members that deal with moral relativism in light of Jesus' teaching and the teachings of the Church.

- Ask leaders from the Catholic school and parish school of religion to plan a fall session for parents on the impact of individualism on family life.

- Invite all parents, coaches, and children who are connected with parish-sponsored sports teams to an afternoon session on "A Balanced View of Sports in a Child's Life."

- Advertise on the parish Web site various weekly recommendations about good television programs for families and which ones to avoid. Arrange for discussion questions for family members after such television episodes have been shown. Check with the Diocesan Communications Office for what is available to assist in this endeavor.

- Ask the school principal or coordinator of catechetical activities to plan an in-service day for teachers and catechists to assist them to teach students the knowledge, skills, and attitudes necessary to live in a mobile, changing world.

- Post information about local fear and anger management seminars available from public service agencies in the area.

- Survey parishioners yearly on what they expect of parish leaders by way of spiritual, liturgical, and ministerial leadership.

- Invite the pastoral council to discuss the advantages of dividing the parish into subgroups, each with a captain who is responsible to help people in their local communities stay better connected with the larger parish.

- Invite newly married couples to attend an afternoon of discussion with seasoned parents on the topic of "Handling Family and Work Pressures."

- Place on the parish Web site information gleaned from knowledgeable parishioners or other sources on "Creative Job-Search Ideas."

- Include on the parish Web site links for the Vatican Web site and the Catholic Network of Volunteer Service as well as Web sites for catechetical and liturgical resources, crisis hot lines, Catholic youth, and general Catholic interests. For the addresses and information on the best sources available, check with the appropriate diocesan offices.

Greater appreciation of the dynamics inherent in American society assists parishes in evangelizing ministries. When these dynamics are known, the direction that a parish takes in its mission and ministry becomes clearer. This is the topic of Chapter Ten.

# 10.

# *Managing the Parish's Vision*

A poorly dressed African American man rang the parish doorbell. Marci, the pastoral associate, saw him outside, but hesitated to answer the door because she was late for an appointment. Reluctantly, she opened it. Before her stood an old man and a woman with disabilities who sat on the porch steps. The man identified her as his wife and said his name was Benjamin. He asked if anyone had found his glasses, which he left in church the previous Sunday.

Marci told Benjamin to look in the lost-and-found cupboard in the back of church. As he and his wife left, he thanked the pastoral associate. She watched them struggle up the church steps. Feeling both guilty and concerned, Marci went over to church. When she arrived, they were sitting in the last pew. She asked Benjamin if he found his glasses, and he replied, "No." Marci showed him where to look and Benjamin found them. After a brief conversation he said, "You have been nice to me and my wife. I am not accustomed to such kind treatment. Can we join the parish?"

The following Sunday Marci spotted Benjamin in the vestibule. He said, "Hello, Marci!" Then the old man took an envelope from his pocket. "This donation is for the church. It's all I can afford. I live a mile from here and am tired from walking," he continued. "I can't stay for Mass since I must catch the bus for work. When I get off, I'll attend an evening Mass downtown." Then he left. When Marci opened the envelope, she found a wrinkled dollar bill. For her, it was the most meaningful gift the parish received that Sunday.

The Christian community can learn much from people like Benjamin. His witness to Jesus' love influenced Marci and other parish members. Subsequently, the gift of his personal presence meant more than the money he put into the collection basket.

Benjamin's story reminds us that everyone is impoverished in some way. The poverty may be economic, psychological, spiritual, or physical. Whenever Christians acknowledge their poverty, the Spirit ministers through them.

People's needs vary. Sometimes a simple gesture, like helping someone find a lost pair of glasses, can lead to more. Such opportunities invite us to proclaim Jesus' good news of salvation.

A parish responds to Jesus as a community of disciples when it proclaims its evangelizing mission to the culture in which it is situated. To do this, a parish needs to remain connected with the needs of its parishioners. Effective parishes focus their mission on people, not organizations or buildings. When solidly connected with its parishioners' needs, the parish's mission can more easily focus on serving God's kingdom.

This chapter centers on establishing a perspective for parish ministry linked to the good news of God's kingdom. It considers a Parish's Fundamental Orientation, Style, and Mission; A Parish's Mission Statement; the Parish Planning Process; and Pastoral Suggestions. Effective parishes address the fundamental notions developed here, which are at the heart of carrying out Jesus' call to proclaim the gospel.

## A Parish's Fundamental Orientation, Style, and Mission

Parish ministry is influenced by a parish's fundamental orientation (its attitude) and style, which must be considered before addressing the parish mission statement. This section looks at a parish's fundamental orientation, style, and mission.

### Fundamental Orientation

Every parish operates out of a fundamental orientation or attitude that affects its vision, style, and mode of communication. This orientation reflects parishioners' values and indicates why they respond as they do.

The following story illustrates the fundamental orientation of one parish group. St. Patrick's Parish had strong Irish roots. It was built about a hundred years ago by immigrants from Ireland. Every Sunday, male descendents of the parish's founders stand in a circle about fifty feet from the breezeway in front of the church.

One Sunday, it was raining very hard. As Father Stan, the newly appointed pastor, walked from the rectory to the church, he saw about ten older and middle-aged men along with several teenagers and young boys standing in the circle where they always stood before Mass. The rain poured down on them and no one had an umbrella. Still, they stood and talked.

The priest approached, walking under his umbrella and extending greetings. Seeing them drenched, Father Stan said, "It's raining very hard. Why don't you stand under the breezeway in front of church? There you will stay dry." After he spoke, an elderly Irish man replied forcibly, "We know it's raining, but we intend to stay right here. Our ancestors stood in this very spot every Sunday for fifty-seven years. A little rain isn't going to make us to move from here." Somewhat confused, Father Stan shrugged his shoulders and walked toward church.

Seeing him leave, a younger man said, "Father, would you come back here for a moment. We have some explaining to do." When he returned, the man continued, "You don't understand, do you?" Father Stan replied, "No, I don't get it." Then the man continued, "When our Irish ancestors built this church, they constructed a drinking fountain in the middle of the circle where we now stand. For generations our grandfathers, fathers, sons, and grandsons stood around the drinking fountain each Sunday before the eleven o'clock Mass. Here, they laughed, cried, and supported one another. About thirty years ago the fountain broke, and several Irish contractors repaired it. Last summer, unknown to us, it broke again. This time no one informed us, but during the week the parish leaders decided to tear out the fountain and blacktop over it."

The elderly man, who had spoken first continued, "I apologize for my rudeness when you first approached us. Now I am settled down. But I will tell you that no one can force us off this spot. They can tear down our fountain and black top over it. It can rain or snow, but we will not move from here. This is our sacred space, which reminds of where we came from and who we are. Here, we tell our young boys their family histories and what it takes to be a man. We are here on this spot to stay."

Father Stan thanked them for the explanation and said, "I'll see you in church in twenty minutes." That Sunday, many sopping-wet Irish men and boys received communion. As each one received his Lord, Father Stan smiled.

Parishes or groups within a parish act out their fundamental orientations through rituals. The ritual surrounding the water fountain celebrated the fundamental attitudes of these Irish men. The same applies to the ritual patterns of a parish as a whole.

Attempting to put into words the unspoken orientations of Catholic parishes, Avery Cardinal Dulles, in *Models of the Church,* described five models or fundamental orientations of the Church. These are: *community* (deeper relational dimensions of the assembly), *institution* (organization and management), *service* (outreach to the needy within and beyond the assembly), *sacrament* (liturgical dimensions), and *herald* (evangelizing, catechizing, and proclaiming the Word). Some parishes emphasize one of these more than the others, although all are present in every parish. No single model is adequate to maintain a healthy parish.

Different parishes reflect different fundamental orientations. One reflects an institutional attitude; another, a service or proclamation orientation; still another, a communal or sacramental approach. Different orientations may also exist within the same parish, for parishioners differ in their expectations. Regardless of personal preferences, parishioners can join together under the banner of the kingdom of God, the unifying point of all ministries. When this happens, each person contributes his or her gifts to bring alive the kingdom. Love, justice, truth, and forgiveness underlie all parish ministries.

## Style

Each parish develops a "style" that responds to its fundamental orientation. This style mirrors its story, ethnic composition, socioeconomic status, size, location, personal and physical resources, and leadership. The report *Parish Life in the United States* discusses the following parish styles:

*Organizational.* This parish, often large in membership, has numerous commissions, meetings, programs, and activities. These allow many people to engage in a variety of activities. Such parishes have many things happening and employ an adequate staff.

*Hospitality.* This quality helps people feel welcome and at home. It encourages self-initiated activities by parishioners and invites them to assume responsibility for creating a welcoming Christian community.

*Formation/evangelization.* These parishes focus on issues related to faith growth. They emphasize liturgy, sacramental programs, catechesis, retreats, and prayer experiences.

*Social action.* While not limited to poor areas, this style often is found in poorer communities. It stresses social services, community development, housing, health, and communal networking.

*Service.* These parishes focus on attending to the needs of individual members. Such needs include counseling, personal support, and various other services. Parishioners are known by name, and the staff is available for parish, home, and hospital visitation.

*Culture carriers.* These national parishes emphasize sustaining the traditions of particular social or ethnic groups.

*Parish Life* says, "There are many other styles and most parishes probably combine two of these styles. An excellent parish may include all of them. The point is that there is no one good style. The style should suit the needs of the people and is influenced by the preferences of the pastor and other leadership" (p. 6). This report reminds a parish that its mission statement and pastoral plan needs to be based on the parish's unique orientation and style.

All parish administrators, especially pastors, are responsible for establishing a parish perspective with the kingdom of God as its ultimate goal. Parish activities and organizations exist to proclaim the kingdom. Coaches, athletic clubs, social groups, housekeepers, and bookkeepers exert strong influence on a parish's orientation. If such influence is positive, it supports parish ministry. If negative, it stifles it.

To minister in light of the kingdom means that parish ministers, including the pastor and staff, agree on priorities. Stressing the pastoral approach does not disparage the importance of policies or rules that assist in the orderly carrying out of the parish's mission. The pastoral approach does not downplay the importance of good administration, which is necessary to identify, call forth, organize, and support the gifts of the community. Good management, organization, and planning help fulfill the parish's obligation to bring God's kingdom to fulfillment. Without competent management, good ideas rarely get off the drawing board, and parishioners experience frustration. Effective administrative models flow from the parish's style. What works in a rural Kansas parish may fail in suburban Atlanta or inner-city Chicago. The one constant in all parishes is the kingdom of God. With this, an administrative structure gives life; without it, a parish is little more than a social agency.

Hospitality is central to any effective parish. In this regard, Deacon Ed said, "In our parish we have greeters at all the doors welcoming people to the parish. The greeters are different from the ushers. At the beginning of each weekend Mass, people are asked to take a moment to introduce himself or herself to someone whom they don't know. The priest walks down from the presider's chair and seeks out someone *he* does not know. Our community formation committee of the pastoral council has a reception twice a year for new parishioners, who get personal invitations. For those whose names we don't yet know, we make an announcement at Mass that they, too, are welcome to come. The pastor sends out letters each month to anyone, Catholic or not, who has moved into the neighborhood to welcome them. He averages about fifteen letters each week." Although each parish handles hospitality differently, this facet of a parish's style is very important for successful ministry.

## Mission

The Father sent Jesus to announce the good news of God's kingdom. This kingdom exists in the "now" of our present lives and will be fulfilled in the kingdom of the "not yet" in heaven. God's kingdom exists everywhere that God is present. It focuses on addressing people's physical, psychological, spiritual, and economic needs. When we reach out to a grieving friend, a disappointed colleague, or a sick child we reflect the kingdom in action. Proclaiming the kingdom is every Catholic's mission.

Jesus taught us that God's healing presence can help people overcome the poverty and evils resulting from sin and the world's imperfections. This healing presence binds up the broken, reconciles sinners, and brings hope. Ministers of the kingdom may not be able to cure a person's physical or economic condition, but through listening and compassion they help them experience inner healing.

Jesus' mission reached its completion in his suffering and death, the price he paid for our sins. His resurrection assures us that he has reconciled humankind with God, and that we can achieve limited happiness here and eternal salvation hereafter. The love we show to a suffering person witnesses the living presence of the risen Lord's Spirit. Such testimony speaks of a world beyond suffering where there are no more tears or sorrow.

Pentecost gave birth to the Church. When the Spirit descended upon the disciples in tongues of fire, they saw in a new way. This first Christian community recognized that Jesus was not dead, but that he lived in them through the power of his Spirit. This great insight changed them. No longer were they fearful, for the Risen Lord continued to live among them. The first disciples became bold witnesses of the faith as they continued Jesus' mission of salvation through their lives and ministry. His mission became their mission, and their ministry reflected his ministry.

## A Parish's Mission Statement

A parish develops its mission statement to make explicit its call to serve God's people. This statement, acknowledging the parish's responsibility at this time and in this place, flows directly from Jesus' mission. It expresses the parish's acceptance of its mission and encourages parish ministers and parishioners to accept the parish's mission as their own. It focuses on the call to discipleship and encourages parishioners to act as Jesus did through the ministries of Word, worship, and service. *Parishes and Parish Ministers* recognizes the significance of the parish mission statement when it says, "It appears that parishes are trying to become more intentional, organized, and participative in their ministry. Half the parishes have adopted a mission statement, whereas five years earlier, only 29.3% had such a statement" (p. 14).

A parish mission statement may change as the parish community refocuses its direction. This happened at St.

Mark Parish within a period of three years, as parish demographic and ethnic composition shifted, leadership changed, and the parish school assumed new responsibilities. Their two mission statements show the changes. This was its first statement:

> St. Mark Parish is a Christ-centered, welcoming community grounded in the Catholic Christian tradition, whose members seek to fulfill the challenge of loving God and our neighbors as ourselves.
>
> In order to meet this challenge we join together to share our faith and to advance the spiritual, educational, and social development of the greater community.
>
> In faithfulness to God's commandment, we accept the call to Christian witness and social action.

Three years later, the parish reformulated its mission statement to read:

> St. Mark Parish is a welcoming community grounded in the Catholic Christian tradition, whose members strive to nurture a closer relationship with God and others. We believe that every member is called to participate in the growth of community through their gifts of time, talent and treasure. In an effort to witness to our faith in all aspects of our lives and community, we join together to develop ourselves spiritually, educationally and socially.

The second statement reflects changing parish composition and leadership. While retaining the basic thrust of the earlier statement, the latter stressed the responsibility to share time, talent, and treasure. It also emphasizes educational developments. This mission statement established the overarching perspective for parish ministries, addressing every member's role and focusing on education. These are important in developing St. Mark Parish's five-year pastoral or ministerial plan and in establishing the goals and objectives that emerge from this plan.

A parish's mission statement takes into account its size, shape, ethnic composition, and unique needs. Distinctive characteristics of each parish influence its mission statement, which helps a parish see the kind of leadership and organization it needs. The pastor in a northern city reflected on changes in parish life during the past thirty years. He remarked, "Being a pastor today is different from when I was ordained. Early in my priesthood, I attended all wedding receptions and went with families to their home after funeral services. No longer can I perform such ministerial tasks, which I see as very important. I am too busy with other parish demands, especially administrative responsibilities. I cannot physically minister one-on-one to parishioners, as I once did. The best I can do is to help develop a solid mission statement, encourage lay ministry, celebrate well at liturgical functions, attend necessary meetings, support the parish staff, and pray that parish ministry serves individual parishioner's needs." In developing a mission statement a parish needs to acknowledge the pressures reflected in his words.

Parish leaders also must acknowledge the tensions that underlie ministry in a secular, speed-oriented, pressurized world. Living in a highly sophisticated, computerized society, parishioners want the parish to respond to them as persons. They expect it to address their spiritual needs, listen to their stories, and return their phone calls. There is no easy way for a parish to satisfy such wants and also to present the gospel message effectively.

Certain things are clear. An effective parish responds to the immediate needs of hurting parishioners. Parishioners are blessed when they receive consolation in their time of need, especially at key life moments such as sickness and death. It is distressing when no response comes. This happened when a woman asked for assistance at the death of her husband. No one except the funeral director called her before or after the funeral, even though she left several messages on the rectory answering machine.

Father Jim told how an experience with a grieving family taught him to be attentive during rites of passage in people's lives. He said that a funeral director asked him to conduct a wake service at the funeral parlor for Fred, a deceased lapsed-Catholic. The priest learned that he had left the Catholic Church forty-eight years before. From that time on, neither Fred nor anyone in his family attended church. But out of deference to his Catholic past, his wife requested that a priest conduct the service at the funeral home.

After receiving the telephone call from the funeral director, Father Jim called the widow. She and her family were overwhelmed with gratitude after he expressed his condolences and spoke at length to family members he had never met.

The day of the wake, the family waited for Father Jim at the funeral parlor. The widow said, "I could not wait to meet the priest who was so kind to us." The ceremony that ensued was a beautiful farewell to a good man.

When the funeral director closed the casket, the family gathered in the hall, preparing to go to the gravesite. Suddenly the widow became very disturbed. She cried out, "We have to go back; we forgot something." Her son said,

"What, Mom?" Distressed, she answered, "Where is his rosary? We forgot to put Fred's rosary in the coffin with him. Where is it? Where is it? Hold up the funeral procession."

Anxiously, her children said, "Mom, we don't have the rosary." She replied, "We cannot proceed until we find the rosary. Go out to the truck and see if it's there." In a few minutes, her son returned with the rosary. The funeral director opened the casket, and she gently put it between her husband's fingers.

At peace, she said to those assembled, "It's now time to lay Fred to rest. Every day of his life, he faithfully said his rosary. As his pipeline to God, it will take him straight into heaven. Now the rosary is in Fred's hands, where it belongs, and Fred is in God's hands." Then the mourners went to the gravesite to lay Fred to rest. This experience indelibly etched on Father Jim's mind the importance of personal ministry. One simple phone call made a tremendous difference. Something similar can happen every time Christians reach out in compassion to hurting people.

Today's Catholic parishes change as they consolidate, merge, or cluster. As *Parishes and Parish Ministers* says, "Some parishes are also being merged or clustered (17% report that they are part of a cluster) and parish ministers are being called upon to serve more than one parish as is true for a growing number of priests. This calls for considerable energy, flexibility, and readiness to relate to a variety of parishioners" (p. 20).

As Catholic parishes shift focus, parishioners still expect spiritual assistance to counter the relativism, materialism, amorality, and impersonalism they experience in society. Some in our Catholic community wonder if large parishes can provide adequate spiritual ministry. Seen through the eyes of Protestant megachurches, the answer is, "Yes." With good leadership, preaching, and liturgy, the latter attract new members weekly. The same can happen in Catholic parishes. Parish leaders are challenged to do their best to get to know the names and faces of parishioners. Personal recognition goes a long way in making people feel at home.

*Parishes and Parish Ministers* addresses the issue of larger parishes in the words, "Parishes are getting larger while smaller percentages of parishioners are participating in the Eucharist on a given Sunday. Consequently, parishes need both good structures for organizing their ministries to serve large numbers of parishioners and to engage parishioners more personally in a community of faith" (p. 20).

Catholics want their parish to be more than impersonal, efficient, organized, and financially solvent institutions. They expect a community setting where they honor God and address their spiritual needs. Providing this atmosphere challenges parish leaders to develop a sense of ministry in all parishioners and all through the organization.

Regardless of the parish's size, demographics, location, economic condition, or ethnic composition, it needs to acknowledge the deep, inner tensions present when witnessing effectively to Jesus' message and meeting parishioner's spiritual needs. It is especially important to keep attuned to their spiritual needs at key moments in their lives, such as marriage, sickness, and death.

Sometimes, parishes do not recognize how deep parishioner unrest goes. Jill, a pastoral minister at St. Lucy's Parish, said that many active parishioners stopped coming and now attend non-Catholic denominations. She said, "Sometimes people, especially youth and young adults, find the message and style of Catholic parishes boring or irrelevant. They look for spirituality that touches their lives. Some drop out completely or seek other avenues of worship in New Age churches in rented spaces, hotels, or shopping centers."

Jill knew how parishioners perceived St. Lucy's. With such knowledge, the parish developed a hope-filled mission statement and ministerial plan centered in the Catholic tradition and adapted to contemporary needs. This new parish plan did not overturn existing parish structures, organizations, and programs. On the contrary, they were starting points for the parish's new ministerial delivery system that refocused the gospel in fresh, vibrant ways. This can happen within any parish—rich or poor, urban or suburban, large or small, homogeneous or ethnically diverse.

## The Parish Planning Process

The parish planning process establishes a concrete plan to implement the mission statement. The goals, objectives, and strategies address how the parish internalizes its mission. In an inner-city parish, they may focus on social outreach. In suburban parishes, they may emphasize young families or singles. Their direction rests on the ability of parish leaders to acknowledge real needs, prioritize them, and develop parish ministries in light of them.

Effective parish plans address spiritual needs in light of current social situations. These plans emphasize positive values like freedom, compassion, and altruism, and address negative ones like easy divorce, abortion, individualism, and secularism. In so doing, parishes ought to keep in mind certain points when developing and implementing their parish plans.

- Begin the planning process by asking, "What is the best way for our pastoral plan to connect with the parishioners' core values and spiritual needs?" How a parish addresses this question affects the way it provides meaningful spiritual sustenance for parishioners.

• Focus parish priorities on spiritual renewal as a prime commitment, concentrating on getting to know and love the scriptures as well as developing small faith communities. The help of the Holy Spirit grounds all parish efforts to address people's spiritual needs. This means that a parish centers its pastoral plan on spiritual needs, especially liturgy, prayer, scripture studies, and catechesis. It also means that the parish's ministry pays particular attention to teenagers, singles, young adults, and families No parish flourishes unless it centers on the spiritual needs of people.

The parish is not primarily responsible for parishioner's physical, social, or athletic needs. This does not imply that it ought to stop giving food or clothing to needy people or that it no longer sponsors dances, social activities, or sporting activities for children, youth, and adults. These are fruitful means to evangelize and solidify community relationships. But social and athletic programs cannot be a parish's chief priorities. They are valuable only if they contribute to the parish mission of proclaiming Jesus' good news.

• Emphasize the ministries of Word (preaching and catechesis), worship (liturgy and prayer), and service (addressing peoples' needs through the healing message of the gospels). Effective parishes provide multiple ministerial opportunities, including vibrant religious education, living liturgies, social outreach, and ecumenical and interreligious dialogue. The effectiveness of such ministries depends on sensitivity to parishioners' cultural contexts, which set the agenda for people's lives, affect their search for meaning, and open up new avenues for parish service. Such ministry begins by addressing individual and family needs. Meeting them requires community effort, for no individual possesses the skills, energy, or time to respond to a parish's multiple needs.

Religious instruction is not limited to "teaching about" Jesus and the Church, memorizing prayers, or insisting on exact credal formulas. While important in themselves, these are catechetically incomplete if they fail to include a formational dimension.

When considering liturgy's role in spiritual formation, effective parishes know that liturgy involves more than carrying out the rubrics. It cannot bring people to the Lord without addressing where they are on their faith journey.

● Commit leaders, especially the pastor and parish ministers, to parish spiritual renewal, since parish renewal centers on sharing our belief that God loves us and that we are to love one another. Without the Spirit's guidance, parish leaders cannot effectively share God's love and satisfy peoples' spiritual hunger. They need to enthusiastically implement the parish's ministerial plan, which accepts Jesus' invitation to bind up the broken and reconcile humankind with God. This sets the tone for financial decisions, organizational development, and pastoral agendas.

The parish plan focuses on those occasions when parishioners need spiritual ministry. This is especially important at key rites of passage in their lives, some of which can be anticipated, others cannot. When developing or implementing the plan, ministers are sensitive to such occasions.

• Consider functional activities, like finances, organizations, and maintenance, as means to accomplish the parish's spiritual mission. Effective parishes keep this in mind when developing a budget, for the budget mirrors what goes on in the parish. It suggests a parish's priorities because in a certain sense every budget is a ministry statement.

• Study effective parishes and congregations and see how they accomplish their mission and ministry. Excellent Catholic parishes can be found in every part of the United States. Much can be learned from them and other Christian congregations in the area. Parish representatives can visit them to discover new ministerial approaches and discuss them with leaders of these congregations.

The *Parish Life Report* identifies major directions that effective parishes have taken. Such parishes identify parishioners' needs, strive for ministerial integration, and integrate enthusiasm into parish life. They acknowledge parishioners' need for wholeness, intimacy, personalized faith, and community. These are the starting points for a parish mission that includes ministry to children, youth, adults, and families, as well as parish planning, budgeting, and hiring.

Such parishes develop the basics of Catholic life while remaining open to change. The basics include scripture study, good liturgy and prayer experiences, social ministry, and solid catechesis. Without these Catholic fundamentals, little long-term parish growth happens. Excellent parishes devise ways to connect these basics with parishioners' needs. *Parish Life* reports that parish effectiveness depends on how a parish structures its life and ministry, not on its size, location, language, income, or the presence of a school (p. 17).

● Remember that the pastor is central in parish ministerial efforts. He works with parish personnel to inspire a Christian spirit. He is the "keeper of the parish vision," which he embodies in his person and actions. The pastor is in frequent contact with parishioners and the parish staff, especially those responsible for the ministries of catechesis, liturgy, and service.

● Keep in mind that all parish activities and organizations further the pastoral mission of Christ and the Church. Jesus ministers through the entire community of believers. Consequently, all parishioners work to develop a pastoral orientation in the parish.

● Build into the pastoral plan a reminder that effective parishes take seriously the factors liturgy and preaching, the need to help people deal with practical concerns, especially those pertaining to their children, a democratic leadership style, and an active quality of parish life (*Parish Life,* p. 17).

● Remember that the finance council, the building committee, and the athletic committee serve the chief ministries of the parish, not vice versa. Hence, the parish's mission statement influences the way it spends money. Without a clear commitment to ministry, a parish's pastoral responsibilities can be overshadowed by monetary concerns.

• Develop a unique pastoral plan, since every parish varies in style, tone, size, and composition. Parishes range from large to small, rich to poor. Some have abundant personnel, others lack adequate staff. Regardless of parish configuration, it is important that its ministerial structures are consistent with its style. Otherwise, conflict, tension, and hurts arise and ministry is impeded.

In developing a pastoral plan, do not pattern it too closely on a business model. Such a pastoral model may be efficient, but may not be pastorally effective. The flexibility required for effective ministry cannot be contained in any organizational model, especially one that is highly functional. This simple fact of pastoral service has to be considered if ministers working for the church are to be effective.

A parish's attitudes, perceptions, and expectations affect its approach to pastoral planning, which cannot include solutions for all parish needs. It can, however, suggest ways for the parish to become a ministerial community as well as a clearinghouse to help people utilize services afforded by government agencies and other community support systems.

All Catholic parishes move toward the same goal of proclaiming God's kingdom. This includes developing their own ministries and participating in ecumenical and interreligious ministerial efforts, such as soup kitchens or social justice outreach. For this to happen, parishes need a faith-filled, flexible, future-oriented ministerial plan, rooted in the scriptures, faithful to the Church's teaching, and focused on peoples' needs.

The pastor along with the parish staff set the tone for such a plan. Their leadership inspires parishioners who are the heart and soul of any parish. When this happens, the entire parish becomes a living witness that the Risen Lord is alive in his people.

## Pastoral Suggestions

- Ask the parish staff to plan a study day for all parish ministers focusing on major parish rituals (liturgy, sports, service activities, volunteer ministries). The goal of the day is to discern how these activities complement the parish's fundamental orientation, attitudes, and style.

- Establish an ad hoc committee to develop a process to evaluate how parishioners and visitors regard parish hospitality, most notably at liturgical celebrations and various ministerial functions, as well as in the pastoral center, school, and rectory.

- Plan a series of small parish retreats at a suitable place and time, centering on the faith and spiritual growth of the laity, to be followed up by the establishment of small faith communities.

- Invite members of non–Caucasian ethnic groups to evaluate how the parish welcomes them, invites them to participate in parish ministry, and addresses their needs.

- Plan a town hall meeting centering on How the parish is living out its mission statement.

- If the parish does not have a mission statement and/or a pastoral plan, ask a member of the staff to get the pastor's permission to form a committee to begin the process of developing one.

- Encourage the pastoral council to evaluate the parish's ministerial plan, revise it, or develop a new one, if no plan exists.

Catholic parishes need a focus. Without one, it is difficult to address people's changing needs. This focus flows from its mission statement, which keeps the community on track and allows it to deal with problems that every parish faces. As parish members formulate the parish mission statement, they take more seriously their ownership of the parish. In so doing, planning and implementing the ministerial plan also becomes the parishioner's task, not the job of the priest and ministerial staff alone. New life can come to the parish through this endeavor. This is the focus of Chapter Eleven, which discusses refocusing a parish through rites of passage in people's lives.

# 11.

# *Refocusing Parish Ministries through Rites of Passage*

On Holy Thursday, 2002, Mom's death was approaching. She rested peacefully in her bed, not stirring, a rosary in her right hand and a crucifix in her left. Her whole body, including her head and limbs, never moved during this time. Her skin was smooth and a gentle glow radiated from her. Mom could no longer swallow and breathed heavily through her mouth. Her large hospital room at the end of the corridor enabled ten to fifteen people to sit and stand comfortably around her bed. As evening approached, the number grew.

The atmosphere in Mom's room became more sacred as the day wore on. Anyone entering it experienced a sense of holiness that emanated from her. Several family members commented that we were in a sacred space. A friend expressed our feelings when she said, "Bob, we won't get to Holy Thursday services this year, but we are experiencing the Last Supper right in this room. Look at your mom. She is our Eucharist tonight." As I observed Mom and our family around her bed, I knew more fully what Jesus and his disciples experienced at the Last Supper. The place we were was holy ground.

We arranged a brief prayer service and listened to several readings from the Holy Thursday liturgy. When I gave a tiny sliver of host to Mom on a spoon as viaticum, I knew it would be the last time that she would receive her Lord before she would see him face to face in heaven. How appropriate that it was on the same night that Jesus gathered with his disciples for the last time before he died!

On Good Friday, with her family around her bed from twelve to three, Mom became even more peaceful. She died at seven o'clock. Her death was the most powerful rite of passage our family ever experienced. This sacred happening changed all those who witnessed it. Her death convinced me even more of the importance of key life moments that touch the fiber of our being.

Witnessing Mom's last hours motivated me to refocus on such experiences as central to pastoral ministry. These experiences offer a way to revitalize parishes by concentrating on what is really important. The parish is entering a new era and has the opportunity to become a dynamic presence in a society that hungers for meaning. Recent Church documents, emphasizing evangelization, suggest that parishes need to concentrate on spiritual renewal motivated by real-life experiences. Such renewal does not minimize what is now in place nor does it require new structures. Rather, it demands something more difficult and long range. It asks parishes to develop a "new attitude," a new way of acting as a parish.

Structures are easier to change than attitudes. The latter requires a change of heart as we turn our lives over to the Lord and respond to him in our family, workplace, and parish. Without such renewal, secularism and individualism erode the fabric of society and Church.

Vibrant parishes concentrate on ongoing spiritual renewal, which focuses on the "basics," especially Jesus' call to discipleship. These parishes emphasize giving praise to the God who made us, blesses us, and invites us to be grateful through our prayers and lifestyle. These parishes help us see that whenever we reach out to the least of our brothers and sisters, we honor God. They encourage communal and individual attitudes that zero in on people's needs as fruitful opportunities to proclaim Jesus' message.

This chapter recognizes evangelization as the unifier of all parish ministries. It encourages a parish to reconsider its attitude toward ministry while maintaining its present programs, organization, and structures. The chapter is divided into four parts, Meeting People's Basic Spiritual Needs, Key Life Moments and Sacramental Ministry, Key Life Moments and Extra-Sacramental Ministry, and Pastoral Suggestions.

## Meeting People's Basic Spiritual Needs

Our daily joys and sorrows provide opportunities to grow in a gradual appreciation of God's presence and life's purpose. Key moments, like a birth, wedding, or death, open up deeper avenues for growth. A healthy family and parish environment affords the climate for such growth.

A person's spiritual journey begins in the family. A faith-filled home helps us pray and develop attitudes of right and wrong. In family life rites of passage are particularly important. These may include a teenager being in a serious accident, a single mother losing her job, a father discovering his son on drugs, a woman giving birth to a child, a young person entering adolescence, or a couple getting married. Since these events represent turning points in life, they involve a kind of vulnerability that other occasions rarely bring. In previous generations, religious and social rituals helped people to cope during life's transition times. In our society, similar rites of passage have ceased, broken down, or assumed a secular form. Without the road map that rites of passage afford, it is more difficult for people when they move into a new life stage.

Some rites of passage like marriage or going to college bring excitement; others, like divorce or job loss, bring fear. But all rites of passage happen at core moments in life. Jesus was sensitive to people at such times. He healed the woman with the issue of blood, journeyed to raise Lazarus from the dead, reached out to Zacchaeus, and forgave the adulterous woman—showing God's love, healing, and forgiveness to all those who needed help, in the time and the place where they needed help. His example invites parishes to respond to the needs around them, ministering where and when occasions present themselves.

Emphasizing rites of passage does not mean that parishes jettison existing programs. Parishes require organized programs but never at the expense of needy people. Some pastoral ministers get so caught up in planning, organizational responsibilities, financial matters, and functional concerns that they miss the real opportunities before them. Therefore, parish leaders must raise the sensitivity of volunteer ministers, the congregation, and parish organizations to the importance of these key times in people's lives in order to move parish ministry to a greater depth.

Every parish organization, structure, building, and meeting exists for the purpose of glorifying God and touching the core dimension of people's lives. Significant rites of passage touch these core human dimensions, thereby manifesting deep connections with life's journey as a whole. If parishes acknowledge this connection, their overall approach to liturgy, Catholic School, social ministry, and catechesis may change.

The life-journey paradigm provides key opportunities to minister, at both sacramental and nonsacramental times. The following sections look at each.

## Key Life Moments and Sacramental Ministry

Life's journey involves many elements. Sometimes, we need the prayerful support of friends and family. At other times, we need the spiritual uplift of the sacraments. Each sacrament can touch a core moment in our lives.

### *Birth and Baptism*

Parishes can learn when a parishioner's child is born from a hospital communication or from previous requests for such information in the bulletin. Parents, family members, or friends also may be asked to call the parish secretary after a child's birth. Cards to be filled out with this information can be made available in the back of church.

When parishes receive word of a child's birth, their response can affect the faith development in the child's family. A welcoming response usually bears much fruit. This may include a card to the parents from the pastor, congratulating them on their child's birth, along with a simple religious gift like a statue or plaque. The letter may also include a clarification of the procedures for the child's baptism.

A child's birth invites parish ministers to consider this event as a key rite of passage in a family's life. It initiates a partnership between the parents and parish that can help the parents grow in age, wisdom, and grace. For this reason good baptismal preparation of parents is important. In commenting on such preparation, Father Dave, the long-time pastor of St Lucy's Parish, said, "When people come to have their child baptized, it provides an opportunity for me to interview the couple. This can become a faith moment. A parish secretary should only be the means to connect parents with the priest before anything is decided about the baptism."

Years ago, Jason and Karen, a young couple, set up an appointment with Father Dave to talk about their child's baptism. Karen told him that they were not practicing their Catholic faith. He said, "If you are serious about beginning to practicing it, and tell me so, I will baptize your child after a good preparation on your part. If you allow your child to do so, *she* will teach *you* how to be good Catholics." Today, Jason and Karen are active parish ministers and their children are strong Catholics.

A child's birth is not a once-and-for-all sacramental event, but initiates a life-long process of a whole family's coming to faith. It is an opportunity to help parents see their child's baptism as a key rite of passage leading *them* to a fuller Catholic life. Many pastoral ministers find that if they personally invite parents to attend Sunday Mass, they will respond positively. But baptism is just the beginning of the parish's ministry to families. The ministry requires follow-up, so that parents can learn more about a child's religious growth than is offered in the baptismal preparation program. It also involves ongoing ministry to families, parents, and preschool children.

Jason and Karen's story indicates the importance of a pastoral minister's sensitivity and his or her responsibility to help parents become the "best teachers of their child." Father Dave also recognized the importance of peer ministry when dealing with first-time parents. He had another married couple with a similar background meet several times with Jason and Karen to help them prepare for their child's baptism. This gave him the time to observe their response.

## *Confirmation*

Confirmation offers an interesting challenge for parishes. The age when people receive it varies widely from infancy to late adolescence. This uneven approach leaves some parish ministers ambiguous about its purpose and mode of celebration. The U.S. bishops give wide leeway to local churches in setting the age for receiving this sacrament.

Some liturgists and catechists urge the Church to restore confirmation to its order in the rites of Christian initiation placing it after baptism and before the Eucharist. This ordering, which follows the original sequence for the sacraments of initiation in both Eastern and Western Catholicism, is followed in Eastern Catholic Churches. However, restoring confirmation to its original order by conferring it on children shortly after baptism effectively eliminates confirmation from having real meaning in an adolescent's life. As it has disappeared into baptism, it does not impact upon their religious development.

Many pastoral ministers prefer confirming young people in the seventh, eighth, or ninth grades. This preadolescent age presents an opportunity to address young people from a faith perspective that will show them how their baptism provides a bedrock that helps them face challenges as they mature into adulthood.

While baptism confers the fullness of the Holy Spirit, confirmation offers pastoral ministers and parents the opportunity to remind young people that they are moving into new life dimensions. It is not an initiation rite into adolescence, but a confirmation of the commitment made in their name at baptism. It reminds them of the foundation of their faith. The early Church confirmed the person's baptismal commitment right after baptism. Confirmation now confirms young people's baptismal commitment at a time when they need it. At this time, the Church invites them to freely commit themselves to live their adolescent years in a spirit of faith. With this renewed commitment, adolescents can more confidently embrace the many other rites of passage that they will experience in the coming years. On these occasions, parents and pastoral ministers can help them appreciate how the grace of baptism, confirmed in confirmation, gives them confidence and reminds them of their Christian responsibilities.

Father Bill, a pastor, said, "Confirmation is becoming a problem. Today, many of our adult Catholics are not confirmed. I'm not recommending going back to confirming children when they are about seven. As it is now stands, however, these nonconfirmed Catholics are not fully initiated into the Church. This does not present a problem when they get married, for confirmation is not a requirement for marriage, but becomes problematic when they are asked to be sponsors. It is a requirement for sponsors that they be fully initiated into the Church."

## Eucharist/First Communion

A child's first communion is an important rite of passage in Western Catholicism. Parish ministers are invited to view it in ways that go beyond the child's catechetical preparation and the liturgical celebration. It is a special time to communicate with a child's parents, who often have little knowledge of basic Catholic belief and practice.

First communion allows parish ministers to discuss with parents their own faith. As with baptism, if catechists see first communion as a rite of passage, it is easier to help parents grow in their faith by seeing the significance of the

Eucharist in their own lives. Marietta, a Catholic school principal, commented on the communal nature of the Eucharist: "The celebration of a child's first communion has to be seen as a parish celebration, not a school event. It is an ideal opportunity for children attending the parish school to interact with those attending the school of religion. This does not necessarily mean one celebration. In the last parish that I served, with four hundred children making first communion, this was impossible. We had a dozen celebrations or so in both English and Spanish. This was done at Sunday Masses throughout the month of May. Catholic-school and parish-school-of-religion children were intermingled in all celebrations. In my present parish, with 140 children making their first communion, we have only five celebrations, but the process is the same."

Some parishes, preferring to stress the full incorporation of the child into the community, develop a model whereby parents, catechists, and children prepare for the child's reception of first communion at a regular Sunday liturgy. When this happens, the child or children can receive a special blessing from the congregation, meet the parishioners in the church vestibule following Mass, and be honored afterwards at a regular parish hospitality gathering.

## Reconciliation

The sacrament of reconciliation has little meaning for Catholics who may not have received it for years. Younger parishioners are largely ignorant about its spiritual benefits. Parishes need to emphasize its value in catechetical sessions, liturgical formation programs, and Sunday homilies. They do so by encouraging parishioners to receive it, especially when they need to be reconciled and when they go through rites of passage like engagement, marriage, and departure for military service. Pastoral sensitivity at such times helps make this sacrament an important part of the healing of memories and feelings.

## Marriage

Many engaged couples know little about Church teachings, do not regularly attend Mass, and have no regular parish. As their marriage approaches, they may not know where to begin. Some parents make the initial contact with a parish. Often the couple does it. In any case, marriage is a good time to reach out to these people.

The initial meeting between the engaged couple and a parish minister aims at welcoming them, making them feel good about getting married in this parish, and explaining the procedures necessary to prepare for the wedding. This is especially true when irregular church involvement or mixed religious status makes them hesitant to approach a Catholic minister.

Effective pastoral ministers are encouraged to clarify to the couple that engagement and marriage are important rites of passage. Such ministers stress marriage's spiritual nature. This includes spiritual preparation for the sacrament, the couple's faith life, religion in their home, prayer, and regular Mass attendance. Marriage preparation involves discussions with married couples, engagement retreats, other preparatory sessions, or inventory analyses. In preparing a bride and groom for marriage, pastoral ministers complete the necessary paperwork but stress the couple's readiness and marriage's spiritual dimensions. Deacon Bill, a pastoral associate, offered the following comments about marriage preparation: "A very helpful tool in many dioceses is FOCCUS [Facilitating Open

Couple Communication Understanding Study], an instrument for counseling people in preparation for marriage. It is also helpful to utilize married couples to sponsor the engaged couples in their preparation. Marriage Encounter couples are usually good people to recruit."

Catechetical, liturgical, and service ministers in each parish can be invited to offer input into what is presented in marriage preparation sessions. Without such collaborative efforts the preparation may be one-sided and incomplete. It needs to contain solid biblical, theological, pastoral, and liturgical components. This includes how a spiritual home atmosphere, religious instruction, good example, and family prayer are vital aspects of a parent's Christian vocation. Most parishes need no new ministries to engaged couples but may have to take a look at their existing ministries in new ways.

## Anointing of the Sick

The sacrament of the sick gives physical, emotional, and spiritual healing to seriously ill people and prepares them to undergo surgery or treatment or to enter everlasting life. Such occasions provide the opportunity to touch the sick person deeply and evangelize those present. It may be a life changing moment, as in Sam's case.

Sam was ninety-four and lived at home with his son, Jake. One Sunday Jake returned from Mass and said, "Dad, this morning Father Mike said, 'Because we are baptized, we have the privilege of blessing others.'" Since the old man respected Father Mike, he listened carefully. Some time after Jake finished speaking, Sam asked him to come over to his chair. Sam blessed him and every person who subsequently came into his home.

A month later, Sam became critically ill. It was apparent that he would not recover. Father Mike was called to his home to anoint him. Also present were Sam's other children, grandchildren, and great grandchildren. When all were assembled, they had a beautiful anointing ceremony. After it was completed, Sam spoke faintly, thanked everyone present, and called each one individually to his bed. Beginning with the eldest son and continuing to the youngest great granddaughter, Sam put his hand on each of their heads and blessed them. He died a few days later. The powerful experience of Father Mike's anointing and Sam's blessing evangelized those present.

The sacrament of the sick is often celebrated communally at Mass. At these celebrations the most recent first communicants may give those anointed a rose or other symbol, and the parish community may gather afterward to continue to celebrate their life and enhance the faith of the entire community.

## *Mass of Christian Burial*

Death draws us into the core of life. It connects most intimately with Jesus as the Mass of Christian Burial unites his death with the death of a parishioner, friend, family member, or colleague. Just as Jesus was raised from the dead, so will those who die in Christ be raised to everlasting life with God in heaven.

Since death is the rite of passage par excellence, parish ministers need to be especially sensitive to dying people and to those whose loved ones are near death. When death comes, vibrant parishes are prepared to offer effective bereavement ministry to the loved ones of the deceased person.

Sickness and death are special occasions for evangelization. They give ministers, especially priests, the chance to welcome back lapsed Catholics and to build bridges between alienated family members who may not have spoken with each other in years.

Bereavement ministers perform important functions when death occurs. Father Mike, the pastor mentioned above, said, "Often, bereavement ministers, who may also be Eucharistic ministers to the sick, know the family better than the priest. Sometimes they serve as the presider at vigils or at graveside services."

In addition to preparing for the Mass of Christian Burial and the actual funeral rites, wise pastoral ministers follow up afterward, checking on how the deceased person's family members are doing. Since society is so fast paced, many friends, neighbors, and work associates are ready to move on to the next event soon after a funeral. They may fail to recognize that the grief process is just beginning for those who lost a loved one. Continued parish support offers a welcome beacon for those receiving consolation nowhere else.

## Key Life Moments and Extra-Sacramental Ministry

Certain times and events provide special opportunities to connect the Spirit's workings to rites of passage in people's lives, both good rites of passage and unwelcome ones. Greater awareness of them leads to more effective ministry. Such occasions may include beginning school, discovering a child is taking drugs, graduating from eighth grade, obtaining a driver's license, going to a prom, leaving for college or military service, having a miscarriage, following an abortion, birthing a child with disabilities, getting a divorce, and losing a job and moving away from home.

## Beginning School

While parents usually take great care to provide for their children's safety and education, they sometimes neglect to educate them in the practice of their faith. When children begin school, some of these parents recognize their spiritual obligation to pass on the Catholic faith. A child's entrance into kindergarten or the first grade is a turning point when many parents are open to becoming active parish members. It presents a fine opportunity for parishes to connect on a deeper level with the child's family, especially a parent or parents. A positive attitude may bring some parents into RCIA sessions, Bible study groups, and Christian parenting meetings as well as into personal prayer and deeper spirituality.

Some parishes have certain expectations for parents of elementary school children who attend the Catholic school. These may include regular Mass attendance for Catholics, church involvement for non-Catholics, and suggested attendance at adult formation classes. The latter are recommended for Catholics who know little about their faith.

## Discovering a Child Is Taking Drugs

Drugs devastate families and individuals. Many parents are overwhelmed when they discover that their child is on drugs. Support of friends, neighbors, and parish ministers greatly assists such a family. Drug problems, be they temporary or permanent, provide occasions for parishes to support and comfort people.

Sometimes the drug user is not the child. A catechist or school teacher may discover through a child's disruptive behavior that his or her mother or father or another family member is an alcoholic or on drugs. Even though parish ministers can't solve a family's problem, they can support the family and recommend social agencies or counselors to assist them. Families with similar experiences can also provide valuable assistance to them.

## Graduating from Eighth Grade

Young people look forward to eighth-grade graduation, but many are fearful of beginning high school. This rite of passage is an occasion to help them grow in confidence by supporting, advising, and encouraging them to ask God's help as they move to the next stage of their life journey. As Father Chas said, "Include all parish children in graduation ceremonies—those attending parochial, private, and public schools. Children in private and public schools are often neglected." At eighth-grade graduation, parishes can give each graduate a religious symbol like a rosary or religious medal.

When teenagers enter high school, parishes can maintain contact with them by welcoming them at all parish functions, inviting them to join the parish youth group, requesting their involvement in volunteer projects, and providing them with spiritual and social opportunities. Parishes are encouraged to go out of their way to make high school students feel at home.

## Obtaining a Driver's License

For many teenagers getting a driver's license is the most important event in their high school years. Parishes can use this occasion for fruitful ministry to teenagers by developing a ritual celebration centering on getting the license. Since every parish is different, the style the ritual takes will vary.

Developing such a ritual can begin by organizing and sponsoring a series of parish meetings for parents and teenagers to discuss the challenges and dangers of driving a car. Such meetings discuss the young person's responsibilities, the rights of others, and a teenager's growth to maturity. A team of parents can decide key issues to be addressed, including the right attitude toward driving a car, the issue of drinking and driving, personal responsibility, concern for others while driving, proper behavior in a car, and the morality of reckless driving.

As these meetings progress, parent and teenagers can discuss prayer before each trip, proper conduct with friends or a date in the automobile, road rage, speed limits, and the folly of drinking or using cell phones while driving. Parents need to indicate their willingness to trust their children, and teenagers can promise to be faithful to the contract they will sign with their parents.

The sessions culminate with a ritual during which the teenagers celebrate their getting a driver's license as an important step on their road to Christian maturity. As part of this ceremony, young people pledge to abide by the agreement they sign, parents turn over the car keys to them, and both sign an agreement. The young person agrees to return the car keys if the contract is broken. The teenager also receives some sacred symbol to be put in the car reminding him or her to drive responsibly. The ritual can take place in a church or meeting place, privately or at a special Mass. It often includes a number of teenagers, their parents, families, and friends.

## Going to a Prom

Parish and school ministers can use high school proms as another opportunity to help teenagers accept their growing responsibilities and to remind them that faith makes a difference. At prom time, teenagers are encouraged to reflect on their confirmation commitment, remembering what it means on occasions like this.

## Leaving for College or Military Service

When high school seniors graduate, they usually appreciate a religious symbol like a Bible or crucifix, along with a personal letter from their pastor. The parish can invite them to a special Mass before they leave for college, when the congregation prays for them and sponsors a fellowship gathering in their honor afterward.

Since beginning college is an important rite of passage, it is wise to try to keep in contact with students from the parish. St. Edmund's Parish sends a weekly e-mail communication to every one of its college students. This includes a short prayer, brief reflection on the upcoming Sunday Gospel, and news about the parish. Around Thanksgiving, the students receive an invitation to an informal get-together at the parish for them as well as for any of their friends who are coming home from college or the military service during the Christmas break. This gathering may be particularly attractive for first-year college students who miss their friends and look forward to seeing them again. The invitation tells about the parish-sponsored party, which includes a simple dinner, refreshments, and hospitality. This gives students a positive image of the Church and helps them stay tuned into their faith.

Parish ministers also need to acknowledge men and women entering military service. This, too, is a rite of passage enabling the parish to thank them for their service to our country.

## Having a Miscarriage

Many women bear alone the painful experience of having a miscarriage. Some women and their husbands have found healing in a ritual of passage that helps them grieve for themselves and their deceased child. Parish ministers can raise the issue of possible miscarriage during a marriage preparation session and can develop a ritual of healing for parents who have experienced a miscarriage.

## Following an Abortion

Women who have had an abortion often wish to discuss their situation with a trusted pastoral minister or counselor. Some opportunities to do so exist in pregnancy centers started under Catholic auspices. For example, Project Rachel affords help for post-abortive women in dealing with self-forgiveness as well as right relationships with the Church. An advisor at Project Rachel said, "If abortion isn't a rite of passage, I don't know one." Parish ministers can themselves minister to women who have had abortions or suggest places for them to get spiritual and emotional help.

## Birthing a Child with Disabilities

A mentally, physically, or emotionally challenged child changes a family. The effects such a child produces differs from family to family. Some families cope well, others do not. Some families grow closer, other grow apart. Parents who have a child with disabilities offer parish ministers the chance to extend the love of Christ.

## Getting a Divorce

Divorce affects children of all ages—from babies through college students—and they often blame themselves for their parents' separation. Divorce frays the emotions of everyone involved. Some adults say it is as painful as if the ex-spouse died. There is no finality in divorce, for the other spouse remains alive.

Many divorced Catholics are unsure of their place in the Church. Some feel isolated or wonder about their continued participation in parish life, including the reception of the Eucharist, and their participation in ministry.

Parishes need to show divorced people that the Church cares about them. This type of care goes beyond the established programs for separated and divorced Catholics that are largely psychological and social in nature. Parishes have to provide occasions for divorced people to reflect on their changing lifestyle in light of Jesus' message and the Church's wisdom by offering them spiritual counseling, retreats, or days of reflection. Divorced Catholics hunger for a pastoral response that tells them they are still important, loved, and worthwhile parish members.

## Losing a Job and Moving from Home

Job loss is a significant rite of passage. When people dedicate many years to the same company and their job is downsized or they are let go, the world may seem to crash down around them. Their sudden change in financial security affects all aspects of their life and personal relationships. It may also force physical changes such as selling a home or relocating to another place.

Parishes need to be sensitive to parishioners experiencing job loss who need to move to a new town. This may include blessing them at Mass before they leave town, keeping a record of where they move, and encouraging parishioners to stay in contact with them. A Christmas card or a parish bulletin often means very much to such people who may feel alone in their new location. Even when job loss results in staying in the same geographical area, the trauma involved can be significant. Parishes can develop ministerial responses in such circumstances.

When people move into the parish, parish ministers can celebrate this rite of passage as well with cards, visits, or an occasional Sunday Mass celebration for new parishioners. Similar efforts can thank those who move out of the parish or into a retirement home. Moving to a new location affects more than adult family members. It disrupts the rituals of children and teenagers who have to make new friends, change social patterns, and attend different schools. Parish ministers need to be sensitive to them; by helping them grieve their losses and celebrate new opportunities.

Parishes hold great promise for revitalizing the Catholic spirit and providing a firm anchor in an unstable world. As this happens we need to remember that we are disciples of Christ, sent to proclaim the "good news of Jesus Christ, the Son of God" (Mark 1:1).

## Pastoral Suggestions

Paul Wilkes, in *Excellent Catholic Parishes,* listed eighteen common traits of excellent parishes (pp. 157–67). Each point in this final section begins by quoting Wilkes's common traits as a basis for a checklist. Following each of his quotations, my pastoral questions are intended to help parishes evaluate their life and ministry. Wilkes says that excellent parishes...

1. *Are Looked Upon as Missionary Outposts.*

- To what extent is your parish an integral part of the neighborhood community, seeking to change it for the better while remaining faithful to your Catholic roots?

- To what degree does your parish appreciate its cultural composition, needs, dreams, and customs and take specific steps to address them in preaching and ministry?

2. *Maintain the Edge.*

- How often does your parish evaluate itself, asking how to improve on what is presently being done, especially in the liturgy, to avoid falling into mediocrity?

- If people do not respond enthusiastically to parish ministry, to what extent is your parish eager to change to ensure parish vibrancy?

3. *Have a "Habit of Being."*

- To what extent does your parish manifest a fundamental orientation that reflects welcome, respect, excellent ministries, connections to real life, and a joyful presence in the liturgy and at other times?

- In what ways can it be said of your parish that new attendees and regular members are moved by the enthusiasm and eagerness of parishioners to respond to them as persons, concerned about their faith and human needs?

4. *Are Accepting and Forgiving.*

- In going beyond ordinary hospitality, how does your parish let people know that no matter who they are, what they have done, or what their situation in life is, they are welcome as a part of this parish community?

- To what degree does your parish make people feel that their presence alone is sufficient reason for the community to welcome them and that there are no hurdles to overcome before they are accepted as part of the parish?

5. *Are Innovative and Entrepreneurial.*

- In reaching out to society, including the unchurched, seekers, young adults, and delinquents, to what extent is your parish willing to break new ground in order to meet current needs?

- In what ways does your parish creatively face new challenges, while remaining faithful to Catholic belief practices, and already existing parish structures?

6. *Are Willing to Take Risks.*

- To what extent is your parish stuck in old ways of doing things, and to what degree is it willing to move out of its comfortable rituals of ministry and take risks?

- In what ways does your parish go beyond what is usually expected in various ministries to tread new waters when dealing wisely with issues like tithing or gay Catholics?

7. *Are Willing to Make Mistakes.*

- To what extent is your parish willing to take new paths in order to minister effectively?

- In what ways is your parish's fundamental orientation more comfortable with staying where it is, even when it means a failure to meet new ministerial demands, rather than reaching out for fresh ways to minister?

8. *Apply the Rules, But Apply Them Intelligently.*

- To what extent is your parish's basic perspective one that "goes by the books," insisting on the exact following of rules and policies with little or no consideration of people or pastoral circumstances?

- While not being iconoclastic, to what degree is your parish regarded as one that ministers with an "informed pragmatism" (p. 161)?

9. *Offer Little Place for Ideology and Church Battles.*

- To what degree can your parish address divergent views on matters like the ordination of women and married priests without making those favorable or unfavorable to such issues feel they are not welcome?

- How would you gauge your pastor's and pastoral leaders' ability to diffuse internal squabbles on controversial matters, not allowing them to affect the parish's vitality or its ability to attract new members?

10. *Reflect A Different Kind of Authority.*

- To what extent does the authority in your parish reflect a style that is cooperative, appealing, and encouraging, not one that is heavy handed?

- In what ways do pastoral authorities in your parish respect people's freedom, show integrity in judgment and action, and exercise their responsibilities with prayerful, sensible, and useful action?

11. *Have a Long-Term Pastor.*

- In your parish's experience, how would you judge its ability to maintain the same pastor for a number of years, thus enabling him to create a climate conducive to effective ministry?

- To what degree do your pastoral leaders recognize that growth takes time and requires collaborative effort, while admitting that mistakes will be made when changes occur in the parish?

12. *Are Based around an Idea, a Relationship.*

- In what ways has your parish been able to create an atmosphere where parishioners feel a special bonding to one another, parish leaders, and the parish itself?

- To what extent does your parish's basic orientation account for the need of many people to feel connected with it in a personal way, thus regarding it as "their parish"?

13. *Form the Core of Parishioners' Lives.*

- For how many is your parish a major focal point of their lives and of what they do, a place where other parishioners and leaders give them support, spiritual affirmation, and hope in such a way that they tell others and invite them to attend their wonderful parish?

- To what extent do parishioners take with them into their families, work, and neighborhood—their mission territories—the lessons learned from the parish's catechetical, liturgical, and service ministries?

14. *Are Many Communities within the Community.*

- How does your parish acknowledge that different perspectives, fields of interest, and communities exist within it, thus breaking the impersonalism of a large anonymous parish by addressing the special needs of different groups?

- In what ways does your parish recognize itself as an umbrella under which different peoples assemble for liturgy, while encouraging small parish communities to support divergent interests?

### 15. *Are Enough for All.*

- To what degree does your parish see lay men and women as equals in ministry, acknowledging their individual talents and encouraging them to accept new responsibilities as disciples of Christ?

- How much do the pastor and pastoral staff affirm talents of parish members and call them forth to minister without being threatened by their talents?

### 16. *Believe in Quality.*

- To what extent does your parish pay competitive wages, attract talented staff members, and spend adequate money for quality resource materials, rather than rely on volunteers alone or outdated books and supplies to keep ministries going?

- In what way does your parish study the extent and ways that they use volunteers, so as to maximize their talents, respect their personal and home lives, and avoid burning them out through excessive work?

### 17. *Keep Spirituality at Their Center.*

- In analyzing your parish's orientation, in what ways can you say that the parish has an active spiritual quality about it—that much is going on?

- If your parish exhibits this active quality, how is the parish's main focus on spirituality, centered on the conviction that no ministry or program is really on target unless it is based on prayer and rooted in a spiritual orientation?

18. *Offer an Ascent to God.*

- How can you say that your parish is a place where parishioners experience God's presence and grow with other parishioners in an awareness of that presence?

- To what extent does your parish proclaim in its words, deeds, and spiritual atmosphere (including liturgy, eucharistic adoration, and a prayerful climate) that God lives in parishioners' lives whenever they serve their families, minister to the poor, welcome new neighbors, catechize, or teach children how to pray?

Jesus invites us to go into the harvest and teach the good news. As we minister in Jesus' name, we do well to remember the words of Paul and Barnabas, "For so the Lord has commanded us, saying,

'I have set you to be a light for the Gentiles,
so that you may bring salvation to the ends of the earth.'"
(Acts 13:47)

## Conclusion

As parishes bring the kingdom message to a changing culture, they face new and creative challenges. Internal challenges invite parish ministers to apply the message of the scriptures and the church to an undefined future, where people of different ages, backgrounds, and nations become one in their common concern for survival, justice, compassion, and peace. External challenges invite the parish community to simplify its message, take a look at its priorities, call all Catholics to minister, and give a deep commitment to the poor.

No ministry stands alone. Catechesis flows into liturgical celebration and is directed toward service as parish ministries blend into a unified whole. When this happens, parishioners learn that they are imperfect people, co-travelers on a pilgrim journey. They make mistakes, encounter imperfect parish structures, and discover pastoral ministers with whom they disagree. As people of faith, striving to live their Christian life in a broader community, they are blessed because they respond to the Lord's call, "Come, follow me." Ministry is the responsibility of all parishioners. When Catholics accept this responsibility, it bears fruit.

# Bibliography

References are not repeated in subsequent chapters.
Church documents are available in full online at the
Vatican Web site at www.vatican.va.

## Chapter One

*Code of Canon Law* (Washington, DC: Canon Law Society
of America, 1983). This provides the fundamental eccle-
siastical laws and canonical discipline for the Latin
Catholic Church.

*Our Hearts Were Burning Within Us* (Washington, DC:
USCCB, 1999). This is a pastoral plan for adult faith formation in the United States drawn up by the U.S.
Catholic bishops. The plan emphasizes the call to discipleship and provides many suggestions to enhance ministry with adults.

*Catholicism USA* by Brian T. Froehle and Mary L. Gautier,
in conjunction with the Center for Applied Research in
the Apostolate (Maryknoll, NY: Orbis Books, 2000).
This book gives a portrait of the current Catholic
Church in the United States. It contains information
about the Catholic population, behavior and values of
Catholics, and changes and continuities in Catholic institutions and ministry.

*The Parish in Catholic Tradition* by James A. Coriden
(Mahwah, NJ: Paulist Press, 1997). The author offers
insights on the history, theology, and canon law of local

churches. This clear and succinct book reflects on many key dimensions of today's parish.

## Chapter Two

*Rite of Christian Initiation of Adults* (Chicago: Liturgical Training Publication, 1988). The Rite of Christian Initiation of Adults (RCIA) was prepared by the International Commission on English in the Liturgy and the Bishops Committee on the Liturgy. This book contains the liturgical paradigm of Christian initiation of the restored catechumenate, directed by Vatican II.

*Catechism of the Catholic Church* (Washington, DC: USSCB, 1994 and 1997 [Second edition]). Promulgated by Pope John Paul II, the *Catechism of the Catholic Church* is an official compendium of Catholic belief. It is built on four pillars, namely, the profession of faith, celebration of the Christian mystery, life in Christ, and Christian prayer.

*On the Unicity and Salvific Universality of Jesus Christ and the Church (Dominus Iesus)* (Boston: Pauline Books and Media, 2000). This document, prepared by the Congregation for the Doctrine of the Faith, discusses the definitiveness of the revelation of Jesus, the role of the Holy Spirit, the Church, and the issue of other religions.

*Dogmatic Constitution on the Church (Lumen Gentium)* (Collegeville, MN: Liturgical Press, 1975). The constitution discusses the mystery of the Church, the people of God, the Church's hierarchical structure, the laity, the universal call to holiness, the Church's eschatological nature, and the Blessed Virgin.

*Pastoral Constitution on the Church in the Modern World (Gaudium et Spes)* (Collegeville, MN: Liturgical Press,

1975). This decree discusses the situation of people in the modern world, the dignity of the person, the human community, human activity in the world, the Church in the modern world, and issues of special urgency.

*Welcoming the Stranger Among Us: Unity and Diversity* (Washington, DC: USCCB, 2000). This statement of the United States bishops is offered to the Catholic population as they welcome immigrants and refugees the United States, considering the many points that surround this issue.

*General Directory for Catechesis* (Washington, DC: USCCB, 1997). The *General Directory for Catechesis* is issued by the Congregation for the Clergy and is regarded by many bishops, priests, and catechetical leaders as the definitive work on catechesis since Vatican II. It presents a comprehensive look at catechesis, which it situates within the Church's evangelizing mission.

*The Vocation and the Mission of the Lay Faithful in the Church and the World (Christifideles Laici)* (Washington, DC: USCCB, 1988). In this post-synodal apostolic exhortation, Pope John Paul II discusses the dignity of the lay faithful in the Church, their participation in the Church as communion, their co-responsibility for the Church's mission, stewardship of the Church, and the formation of the laity.

## Chapter Three

*Sons and Daughters of the Light* (Washington, DC: USCCB, 1997). *Sons and Daughters of the Light* is a pastoral plan for ministry with young adults. This document was authorized and approved by the National Conference of Catholic Bishops. It discusses the young adult, the vision of faith, a plan for ministry, the campus, diocesan and Catholic organizations, and the implementation of the pastoral plan.

*Parishes and Parish Ministers* by Philip J. Murnion and David DeLambo (New York: National Pastoral Life Center, 1999). This study of parish lay ministry gives research results of studies about today's parishes, the evolving nature of parish life, who the parish ministers are, and details about entering parish ministry.

## Chapter Four

*Evangelization of the Modern World (Evangelii Nuntiandi,* 1975, Preparatory Document #102). This work is an apostolic exhortation of Pope Paul VI. Many regard this work as the "Magna Carta" of Catholic evangelization. It provided the dynamic impulse for the Church's thrust toward a holistic nature in Catholic evangelization.

*Catholic Evangelization: The Heart of Ministry* by Robert J. Hater (Dubuque, IA: Harcourt Religion Publishers, 2002). This discusses the meaning, role, and distinctive characteristics of Catholic evangelization. It gives a brief history of the word *evangelization,* connects it with creation, family, work, and the parish, and then links it with liturgy, service ministries, and the ministry of the Word.

*Sharing the Light of Faith* (Washington, DC: USCCB, 1979). This is the National Catechetical Directory for Catholics in the United States. Approved by the National Conference of Catholic Bishops and the Sacred Congregation for the Clergy, it provides guidelines for catechesis in the United States, based on the *General Catechetical Directory.*

*Gospel of Life (Evangelium Vitae)* (Boston: Pauline Books and Media, 1995). This encyclical letter of Pope John Paul II considers the Christian message concerning the sacredness of life, threats to human life, and a new culture of human life.

*Crossing the Threshold of Hope* by Pope John Paul II (New York: Alfred A. Knopf, Inc., 1995). The pope reflects on deep theological issues in relation to human life. He discusses his personal beliefs and practices and such issues as God, Jesus, the centrality of salvation, evil in the world, the existence of many religions, Buddhism, Judaism, the new evangelization, human rights, and hope.

## Chapter Five

No new references.

## Chapter Six

*Catechesis in Our Time (Catechesi Tradendae)* (Washington, DC: USCCB, 1979). *Catechesis in Our Time* is an apostolic exhortation of Pope John Paul II that offers guidelines for a pastoral approach to catechesis. Rooted in Jesus as the teacher, the pope discusses catechesis and the Church's pastoral and missionary activity. He considers catechesis and evangelization, forms of catechesis, the need for everyone to be catechized, ways to catechize, and catechesis as a task that concerns every Catholic.

*Justice in the World* (Washington, DC: USCCB, 1971). This work reflects the results of the first World Synod of Bishops in Rome after Vatican II. It considers justice and world society, the gospel message and the mission of the Church, the practice of justice, and a world of hope. This document set the tone for the subsequent thrust of the Church's strong stance for social justice.

*Parish Catechetical Ministry* by Robert J. Hater (Mission Hills, CA: Glencoe Publishing Co., 1986). In this book, Robert J. Hater discusses new challenges and opportunities for parishes, parish catechesis, the mission of Jesus and the Church, significant issues in parish catechesis, and implications for catechesis.

*Sharing Catholic Social Teaching* (Washington, DC: USCCB, 1998). This document contains reflections of the U.S. Catholic bishops and a summary report of the task force on Catholic social teaching and Catholic education. It contains major themes in Catholic social teaching, educational challenges, and directions for the future.

*Parish Life in the United States* (Washington, DC: USCCB, 1982). This is a final report to the bishops of the United States by the Parish Project. It contains a report (including statistics) of the then-current state of parishes in the United States, responses, the service of dioceses, and recommendations for the future of parishes.

*Renewing the Vision: A Framework for Catholic Youth Ministry* by G. Patrick Zieman and Roger L. Schwritz (Washington, DC: USCCB, 1997). Approved by the National Conference of Catholic Bishops, this document offers goals, themes, and components for a comprehensive ministry with adolescents.

## Chapter Seven

*Constitution on the Sacred Liturgy (Sacrosanctum Concilium)* (Collegeville, MN: Liturgical Press, 1975). This document contains general principles for the restoration and promotion of the sacred liturgy. It also discusses the mystery of the Eucharist, other sacraments and sacramentals, the Divine Office, the liturgical year, sacred music, sacred art, and sacred furnishings.

*Excellent Catholic Parishes* by Paul Wilkes (Mahwah, NJ: Paulist Press, 2001). In this book, Paul Wilkes presents a guide to the country's best Catholic parishes and practices. He describes these excellent Catholic parishes, gives common traits that these parishes exhibit, presents a "points of excellence" index, and offers a directory of these excellent parishes.

*On the Eucharist (Ecclesia de Eucharistia)* (Washington, DC: USCCB, 2003). This encyclical letter of Pope John Paul II considers the Eucharist in the context of the mystery of faith, the building of the church community, apostolicity, ecclesial communion, and its dignity as a celebration. It concludes by looking at Mary and the Eucharist.

## Chapter Eight

*In All Things Charity* (Washington, DC: USCCB, 1999). In this statement the U.S. bishops offer a pastoral challenge for our time. It discusses the message of scripture and the teaching of the Church, the response to the call for charity and justice, and topics on the Church, Catholic Charities and civil society, and the challenges of the new millennium.

*Guidelines for the Study and Teaching of the Church's Social Doctrine in the Formation of Priests* (Rome: Vatican Polyglot Press, 1988). This document, issued by the Congregation for Catholic Education, considers issues pertaining to the teaching of Church's social doctrine in Catholic seminaries. It includes texts of official Church documents on social issues that relate to major points discussed by the guidelines.

*I Will Give You Shepherds (Pastores Dabo Vobis)* (Washington, DC: USCCB, 1990). This post-synod pastoral exhortation on the formation of priests by Pope John Paul II looks at societal issues that challenge vocations and conditions that encourage interest in them. He considers the value of celibacy, preparation of future priests, cooperation with the laity, ongoing formation, and other pertinent issues.

*Instruction on Certain Questions Regarding the Collaboration of the Non-Ordained Faithful in the Sacred Ministry of Priests* (Washington, DC: USCCB, 1998). This instruction from Vatican City discusses the common priesthood of the faithful and the ministerial priesthood, the unity and diversity of the ministerial functions, the indispensability of the ordained ministry, and the collaboration of the non-ordained faithful in pastoral ministry.

*A Family Perspective in Church and Society* (Washington, DC: USSCB, 1987). This is a manual for all pastoral leaders, approved by the administrative committee of the National Conference of Catholic Bishops. It was developed by an ad hoc committee on marriage and family life and discusses a family perspective for all ministries, and the development of the elements of a family perspective.

## Chapter Nine

*Church in America (Ecclesia in America)* (Washington, DC: USCCB, 1999). This post-synodal apostolic exhortation of Pope John Paul II focuses on encountering Jesus Christ in America today. It looks at the path of conversion, the path to communion, the path to solidarity, the mission of the Church in America today, and the new evangelization.

*Baltimore Catechism* (New York: Benziger Brothers, 1949). This work is the result of directions of the Third Plenary Council of Baltimore that catechisms be produced to assist in the religious formation of children, youth, and adults. It contains summaries in question-and-answer form of the basic truths of the Catholic faith. Its spirit and style reflects the pre–Vatican II Catholic Church and does not contain many of the developmental directives commissioned by this council.

## *Chapter Ten and Chapter Eleven*

No new references.